PRAISE FOR *CHARISMA1*

C000173048

'Based on decades of experience as a leader and researching leadership, Kevin Murray has written a powerful book packed with pointers on how each of us can improve our leadership effectiveness through becoming more charismatic in our own, personal way. *Charismatic Leadership* is a treasure trove of tips, written in a punchy, easy-to-absorb style, that allows the reader to take stock, reflect and experiment with the insights Kevin shares. A book to enjoy!'
Fields Wicker-Miurin OBE, Co-Founder and Partner, Leaders' Quest

'Charisma is oft regarded as a "you've either got it or you haven't" kind of thing. Kevin Murray's new book shows how everyone can master the skills of charisma to boost their effectiveness, impact and enjoyment at work.'
Ann Francke, CEO, Chartered Management Institute

'This book is a great read and is clear, persuasive and authentic. It immediately debunks the popular definition of charisma and replaces it with a framework that is compelling, memorable and practical. It does what great books do – it clarifies and codifies what you thought to be true but couldn't articulate.'
Andrew Gardner, Chairman, Medvivo

'Kevin Murray writes my "go to" leadership books and this one is no exception. *Charismatic Leadership* is packed with great insight and lots of practical examples of how you can inspire those you lead and how to become a better and more charismatic leader. Highly recommended.'
Stuart Lancaster, Senior Coach, Leinster Rugby

'This book will set the benchmark for leadership of the future. Its simplicity and clear guidance, married to immense insights and experiences, make this book a powerful tool.'
Michael Frohlich, CEO, Ogilvy UK

'Kevin Murray's thoughtful and practical dissection of charisma takes the mystery out of the legend and challenges the reader to find their charisma within. Engaged workforces perform better collectively and are happier individually; they react positively to charismatic leaders, so it's worth finding out how to achieve charismatic leadership by studying this excellent book.'
Chris Satterthwaite, Chairman, Access Intelligence

'Many feel that the word "charismatic" isn't a term they could ever apply to themselves. You are either born charismatic or you aren't. Kevin Murray's book shows that charisma is multi-faceted and that we all indeed can be charismatic. At a time when we need leaders who can win hearts and minds and encourage brave thinking and doing, in the face of unprecedented change and uncertainty, this book is timely and important.'
Jo Parker, COO, Chime

'Leadership is hard, and Kevin Murray's books always provide a great guide to becoming a better leader. We all know that charisma is a core quality of leadership, but what we may not have known is that charisma can be learned. Kevin Murray tells us how in his latest invaluable guide for managers.'
Jeremy Thompson, CEO, Caytoo Sports Marketing Intelligence

'The forensic insights into leadership traits and challenges in this book are hugely impressive, but it is the clear structure that makes it so relevant and practical to anybody playing or seeking a leadership role. Congratulations on another great contribution to management literature.'
Nicholas Harvard Taylor, Founder, Harvard Public Relations

Charismatic Leadership

The skills you can learn to motivate high performance in others

Kevin Murray

KoganPage

First published in Great Britain and the United States in 2020 by Kogan Page Limited

2nd Floor, 45 Gee Street
London
EC1V 3RS
United Kingdom

122 W 27th St, 10th Floor
New York, NY 10001
USA

4737/23 Ansari Road
Daryaganj
New Delhi 110002
India

www.koganpage.com

© Kevin Murray, 2020
Illustrations © Matthew Gould

ISBNs

Hardback	978 1 78966 095 1
Paperback	978 1 78966 097 5
Ebook	978 1 78966 096 8

British Library Cataloguing-in-Publication Data

A CIP record for this book is available from the British Library.

Library of Congress Cataloging-in-Publication Data

Names: Murray, Kevin, author.
Title: Charismatic leadership : the skills you can learn to motivate high
    performance in others / Kevin Murray.
Description: London, United Kingdom ; New York, NY : Kogan Page, [2020] |
    Includes bibliographical references and index.
Identifiers: LCCN 2019053389 (print) | LCCN 2019053390 (ebook) | ISBN
    9781789660975 (paperback) | ISBN 9781789660951 (hardback) | ISBN
    9781789660968 (ebook)
Subjects: LCSH: Leadership. | Charisma (Personality trait) | Communication
    in management. | Employee motivation.
Classification: LCC HD57.7 .M8935 2020 (print) | LCC HD57.7 (ebook) | DDC
    658.4/092–dc23
LC record available at https://lccn.loc.gov/2019053389
LC ebook record available at https://lccn.loc.gov/2019053390

Typeset by Integra Software Services, Pondicherry
Print production managed by Jellyfish
Printed and bound by CPI Group (UK) Ltd, Croydon, CR0 4YY

*This book is dedicated to all managers who want
to be more effective in a world of accelerating change.*

*It is for those who want to be better equipped
to transform situations and lives and achieve more.*

CONTENTS

charisma
(karizma)

A special personal quality or power of an individual making them capable of influencing or inspiring large numbers of people.

Collins English Dictionary

AUTHENTIC

PERSUASIVE

THE CHARISMATIC LEADER

POWERFUL

DRIVEN

WARM

PART ONE

An introduction to charismatic leadership

01

Why you need charisma...
and what this book will teach you

A small improvement in the soft skills of charisma will make a huge difference to employee engagement and to the performance of the team.

You've picked up this book because you're interested in the idea that you can be charismatic. Until now, you probably never even thought about it. Or, if you did, you dismissed the concept because you didn't believe you could possess charisma. You've seen charismatic people, and you're convinced you will never be their equal. You think charisma is a gift, something a chosen few are born with, and not something you could aspire to yourself.

This is simply not so. Everyone is capable of developing charisma, because it stems from skills you can practise and apply. These skills will make you more inspiring, more trustworthy, more magnetic and charming and influential. Charisma is something you learn, not something you're born with. To get the best out of the people who follow you, you need to exhibit more of the behaviours that make people charismatic. If you want to inspire them to performance levels not even they thought they were capable of, the skills of charisma are pivotal to your success. All of these skills are soft skills, and soft skills are in short supply in business, yet easy to learn.

A small improvement in these charismatic soft skills of leaders would make a huge difference to people's engagement, motivation and efficiency. Of course, you need other skills too: technical skills, marketing skills or strategic planning skills. But the truth is, the managers who do best, and progress the most, are those who develop their soft skills. Yet too few companies invest anywhere near enough in this sort of skills training. So, the hard truth is that it's up to you to find ways to get better.

You have the wrong idea about charisma

What you need to focus on most is to develop your leadership charisma. You probably don't see it that way, because, as I've just said, you don't believe you are capable of having charisma. Nor are you aware of the business benefits of charismatic leadership. That's because you have completely the wrong idea about what charisma is, and how to achieve it. After all, you've met or seen charismatic people, and they've filled a room or stage with their presence, lighting up everyone around them, infecting them with enthusiasm and warmth. If I asked you to name charismatic people, you'd probably pick from famous politicians, actors, singers, sports coaches, and perhaps even some global business leaders. In workshops I run, all too frequently the participants name people like Bill Clinton, Winston Churchill, Nelson Mandela, Mother Teresa, Steve Jobs, Martin Luther King, Margaret Thatcher or Jack Welch.

Those people have or had a huge presence. They radiated personality and strength. They had a cause and you could feel their passion for it. Even if you had less well-known people in mind – people in your own social and work circles – you easily recognize those with charisma, and you envy that seemingly natural way they are able to inspire others or make them feel special. They focus on you with a laser-like intensity, and you feel suddenly like you are the most interesting and important person in the world. Their charisma is contagious, and long after they have left, you still feel the energy of their presence and enthusiasm.

Oh no, not me, you say. I can't be like that. So you don't bother. And therein lies a major missed opportunity. If you were to try, and if you were to become just a little more charismatic, it could have a big impact on how people see you as a leader. In today's world we need charisma more than ever. Leadership is about positively influencing emotions and behaviours and aligning those to a great purpose. That's what charismatic leaders do. It is my belief that charismatic leaders also create charismatic teams. Yes, even whole teams can have charisma, and therefore a positive effect on other teams, on customers, indeed, on anyone they rely on for success. Charismatic leaders create extraordinary teams and achieve extraordinary results.

For this, you need '*affective* charisma', in order to have a great *effect*. Affective describes something that has been influenced by emotions or is a result of emotion. Effective describes something that produces a desired result.

It doesn't matter whether you lead a small team, a big department, a huge division or even a giant company. Affective charisma is about getting members of your team to go way beyond what they have to do, because they want to, because they care, and because they believe they personally can make a difference. 'Affective charisma' is emotional, and positively influences the emotions of others. The result of affective charisma is to have a better 'effect' on performance.

Defining charisma

Let me define what affective leadership charisma is. It is a special power that enables you to positively influence followers and inspire their commitment and willing devotion to a common cause. It is about bringing out the best in your followers, because they feel great about themselves.

This charisma oils the wheels of leadership and followership by providing the connecting tissue that unites those who lead with those who follow. This charisma is more accessible than the highly magnetic, awe-inspiring kind you have in mind, and is much more desirable in modern management. This charisma is more about how you make others feel, rather than being about trying to influence how others feel about you. Is also much more focused on delivering great results, rather than delivering great reviews of your personal magnetism and charm.

This book is about how to power up your charisma, in ways that will enable you to super-charge motivation in your team and encourage far higher levels of discretionary effort. Why do I say 'discretionary effort'? Why is that so important? Because the difference between what people *have* to do and what they *want* to do is called discretionary effort (Figure 1.1).

If you are a leader, you need to love this concept because it is all about improving productivity and profits, without adding huge additional cost. Organizations with highly committed people perform better. This is a simple truth, and I give you more detail about this in Chapter 36.

FIGURE 1.1 The performance benefit of discretionary effort

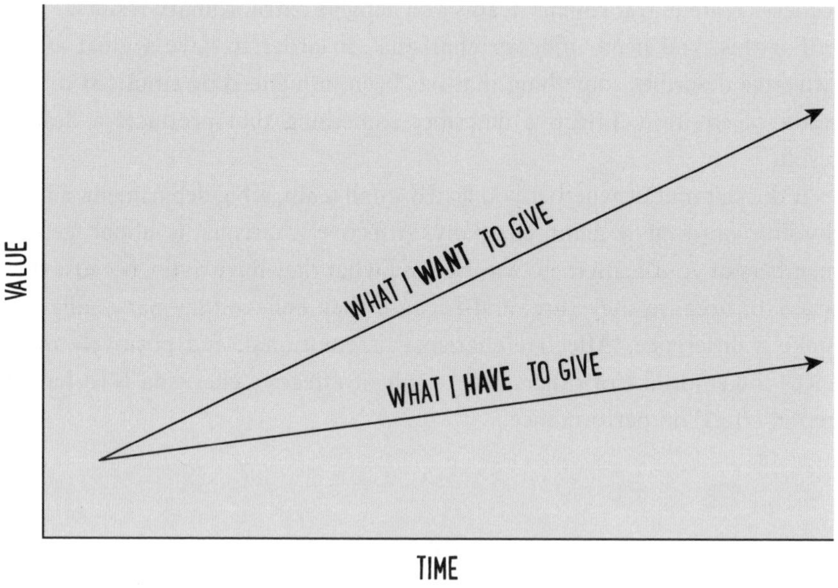

Different kinds of charisma

Without realizing it, I have been studying charismatic leaders for more than 30 years now. I observed that the great ones often had very different kinds of charisma. Some were such authentic people that you just had to love them for their honesty, integrity and principles. Others had a knack of making me feel special and wanting to do better work. Some were so enthused with a purpose that it compelled me to help. Others had a magnetic leadership authority I had no choice but to follow. And others were such eloquent, passionate, persuasive people that I fell under their spell because they managed to connect me to what they wanted to do. Of course, there were those with anti-charisma as well. Smart bosses who managed to repel their followers and, sometimes, incite rebellion.

I have devoted the past 10 years of my life to helping leaders be more inspirational. While researching and writing three books, I have spoken to more than 120 CEOs, conducted various research projects among more than 10,000 managers and employees, and, over the past three years, searched out and devoured everything I could find on charisma.

I have found that there are many kinds of charisma, many different definitions of charisma, and many different ways that each of us can display charisma. And that's part of the problem. For many of us, charisma seems somehow unattainable – gifted to a few lucky people who have it naturally in abundance.

Through this book, I want to help us come to a simple view about what charismatic leadership is, why it matters, and what we can do to be more so, and therefore more effective as leaders. I also want to show that charisma is contextual. There will be times when you need to keep it quiet, and there will be times when you need to switch it on. It will depend on the circumstances.

The traits and skills of charismatic leadership

There are five **traits** that charismatic leaders display. They are:

- authenticity;
- personal power;
- warmth;
- drive; and
- persuasiveness.

A trait is defined as habitual patterns of behaviour, thought and emotion. Those habitual behaviours require **skills** if they are to be *affective* and *effective*. Each charisma trait has five key skills that charismatic leaders can deliver every day in *observable* behaviours:

- Leaders are seen to be authentic if they have the skills to show who they are, as well as to be consistently transparent and principled, and thereby generate trust with and among their followers.
- Leaders who possess personal power have the skills that enable them to be magnetic and more 'followable' as a leader.
- Leaders with warmth have the skills to bring out the best in others by making people feel great about themselves.
- Leaders with drive have the skills to articulate a compelling cause, to which they align everyone.
- Leaders who are persuasive have the skills to hold high-quality conversations which transfer their passion for success to others. They also have the skills to encourage dialogue that powers innovation and progress.

Each of these skill sets delivers a key trait of charisma.

There are enormous business benefits to be had from charismatic leadership behaviours. Employees who benefit from charismatic leaders will:

- Be won over by the authenticity of a leader, and therefore be willing to trust those leaders more. They will also be more inclined to trust others in their teams. Trust is an essential component of successful teamwork and collaboration.

- Feel the influence of a leader's personal authority and be willing to be led.

- Have a greater sense of self-worth, a sense of belonging and a sense of safety – as a result of a leader's warm and affective behaviour.

- Feel listened to, and that their ideas are important. They will be more willing to be creative and go the extra mile.

- Be aligned to a common cause, and crystal-clear about the role they play in delivering it, as a result of their leader's drive and compelling cause.

- Be open to new ideas and constant improvement, and unafraid of change in pursuit of excellence.

- Be highly motivated because of the persuasiveness of their leader, and the clarity that those leaders give. This is important to successful teams, because this encourages robust dialogue, innovation and agility.

Leaders with only moderate levels of charisma can make employees:

- feel more respected, by 65 per cent;

- feel more motivated, by 56 per cent;

- be more likely to see them as inspirational, by 89 per cent;

- be more likely to give discretionary effort, by 24 per cent.

These are bold statements, I know, but the statistics come from some robust research and I will go into this more deeply in Chapter 36. For the moment, however, imagine what a 24 per cent hike in productivity and performance would look like in your team or organization! How much extra profit will that bring? How much extra revenue? How big a leap in customer satisfaction? How much of an improvement in safety performance?

The best news is that you only require moderate levels of charisma to achieve these sorts of results. Too much charisma at work and you could actually have a negative effect on your team. If we power up our charisma to mid-range levels, we can be dramatically more effective. Even better news is that we can all easily learn the skills of charisma and with practice, steadily improve those skills.

What you can learn from this book

In the following chapters, we will look at the chemistry of charisma, and the neurochemical reaction we provoke in followers' brains when we behave in charismatic ways. We will look at why this matters – how it powers better performance in teams and companies. We will look at research on what management behaviours best engage employees and see that these are critical components of management success.

First, over the next five parts of the book, we will explore each of the traits of charismatic leaders, and the five key skills of each trait. These are the skills you need to become a better leader and be more charismatic. Many of these will not only make you a better leader but will also make you more charismatic in your social circles as well. You don't have to try to get better at all 25 at once; I will show you how to prioritize as we go through the five traits of charisma.

In Part Seven we will look at why charismatic leadership is going to grow in importance in a world that is being digitally transformed at breathtaking speeds. I believe that the soft skills of charisma will become critical to collaboration, creativity and success in workplaces all over the world where artificial intelligence, robotics and quantum computing seem to be taking over. Of course, we can't ignore the dark side of charisma, and what bad people do with it, so we will look at the negative effects of warped charisma. I will give you a checklist of what to avoid doing if you don't want to have an anti-charismatic presence.

Finally, in Chapter 37 we will look at a charisma measurement tool, to make it easier for you to work out your own learning programme and priorities, as well as benchmark your progress. In the Appendix you will find this and other tools, as well as a summarized charisma checklist, to help you self-assess or do 360-degree assessments, and focus on what skills of charisma you need to improve to have the most impact.

Charismatic leadership is the result of learning some new behaviours. First, you have to understand what they are and why they are important – and how they can benefit you. Then you need to try some tips that enable you to develop the skills. After that, it is all about practice – lots of practice. Success will breed success and you will travel far. I wish you a productive journey.

02

The five traits of charismatic leaders

With the skills of charisma, leaders can win trust and build loyal teams. They can command more attention and gain respect. They can engage better with people and bring out the best they have to give. They can impart a sense of direction and create a sense of urgency that compels everyone to aligned action. They can connect with people and infuse them with a will to win.

When I ask managers whether they believe that they have charisma, the answer is usually no, especially if I ask them in front of others. A brave few will sometimes admit to having 'a little charisma, perhaps'. The commonly held view about charisma is that it is all about having a huge presence and a powerful magnetism, which, of course, is beyond nearly all of us.

This huge presence and powerful magnetism is not necessarily good for business. In fact, there is strong evidence to suggest that business leaders who are overly charismatic might well be damaging to teams and organizations. The best managers have a quiet charisma, which they apply wisely and appropriately, because they are not driven by the need to be the centre of attention all the time. Charismatic leaders know that they don't need to be awe-inspiring. But they do need to be inspiring.

And that's the point of charisma in business leadership. It's about being able to command attention and build trust. It's about making people feel worthwhile, and that they are valued and important members of a team. Charismatic leaders persuade their teams to their cause and show them where and why they're crucial to delivering it. They give their teams direction and purpose and align the whole team to that common cause. They get people to go beyond what they have to do, to do the very best that they can, because they want to. This is how charismatic leaders achieve great results.

In the previous chapter, we saw that charismatic leaders had to have five traits to make them charismatic. These enable them to:

1 Win the trust of followers. To do this they need skills that will help them deliver **authenticity**.

2 Command attention and win respect. For this, they need the skills that will help them develop **personal power**.

3 Engage with followers and make them feel valued members of the team. To do this they need to develop the skills that will give them **warmth**, and a more affective presence.

4 Impart a sense of direction and urgency. To do this they need to have the skills to articulate a compelling vision and sense of purpose that will arouse the passion to deliver it. Their **drive** comes from a relentless focus on continuous improvement to achieve the goals.

5 Enable them to connect with followers and enthuse them with the will to succeed. To do this, they need to develop their communication skills and become more **persuasive**.

The skills of charismatic leadership

It is no good trying to become brilliant in only one of these areas. It is a blend of these five traits that makes the difference. We will see later that leaders who are strong in one of the skill sets, but weak in others, can actually be destructive as leaders. It is those leaders who are moderately good in all five who are most effective.

In the following pages, I will go into much more detail on each of these five skill sets, and what you need to do to improve on each and every one (see Figure 2.1). I will also show how you can measure your skills now, by self-assessing. More importantly, I will show you how to get others to give you a view on your essential skills of charisma. You won't be asking them to rate your charisma, which would, I admit, immediately make you sound vainglorious. Instead, with more humility, you will be asking them to rate yourself on skills that they will instantly regard as important skills of leadership. Because of this, they will be much more likely to help. By asking a simple set of questions of all members of your team, you will be able to get consistent feedback that will enable you to improve, should you decide to act on what you hear.

You will quickly realize that assessing yourself, if you are brutally honest, will be a reasonable guide to where you need to improve, especially if you rate yourself against some of the scores that I have culled from other leaders. But, the giant flaw in this self-assessment is that you're marking yourself in isolation and others may see you very differently indeed. Those 'others' will be able to give you a good assessment of your skills, because every one of these skills is an 'observable behaviour'. In other words, people will be able to see whether you behave this way, or not. Sometimes, I have seen managers improve in these behaviours simply by being more mindful of the need. That is half the battle.

Let us have a brief look at each of these **traits** and their *skill sets* in turn, consider why they matter so much to the people on the receiving end, and how they will help you as a manager to perform better. This overview will help you navigate your way through the book.

1. Authenticity

The first skill set has to do with being able to display an **authentic** personality. This is an essential part of leadership and it all comes down honesty, integrity, values and respect. People see sincerity straight away, and they will soon sense insincerity or falseness. As a leader you have to gain people's trust in seconds, and you can't do that if you're not authentic. Charisma encourages trust, which enables employees to engage better with charismatic leaders and be more willing to talk with them and express how they feel about things.

Leaders have to focus on building trust, because trust is possibly the single most important element of building effective teams. However, you cannot build trust if people don't trust *you*. To do that, people need to know who you are. They need to know that you know what you're talking about. And they need to believe that you have their best interests – and an honourable cause – at heart. They trust you for your character, your competence and your integrity.

They don't trust you when you remain aloof, hard to read and mysterious. In this case, they will always wonder what your agenda really is and whether you're being completely truthful. More than anything else, this will undermine their willingness to give maximum effort, and they will be inclined always to keep one eye on you and one eye on their work, thus dissolving their focus and effectiveness. Worse still, that wariness will trans-late itself into a lack of willingness to trust colleagues. Once you start a chain reaction of mistrust, you also trigger a lack of respect. A lack of respect translates into a lack of respect for teammates, and for customers. And all of that inevitably leads to disastrous results. When you build trust, you build strong relationships, which lead to better business. The business benefits of trust are enormous.

These are the behaviours you must exhibit in order to be authentic. You need to learn how to:

1 deliver honesty and *integrity*, consistently;

2 have and live a personal set of *values*;

3 be visibly *committed*;

4 be *self-aware*;

5 have *humility*.

You have to be predictable – so clear in your values that people will be able to make decisions when you are not there, knowing what's important to you as a leader and whether or not what they're doing will find favour with you.

This means learning to be transparent, so that people can see you are willing to engage on the things that really matter, no matter how difficult. It means living your values, by being clear about what they are, willing to talk about them openly, and being consistently true to them, thus giving you substance. It means displaying your passion to succeed, in order to transfer it to others. It means being more self-aware, by understanding the beliefs that drive your behaviours, the triggers that cause you to have an emotional reaction, and the impact you have on others. It means under-standing your real strengths and weaknesses and being prepared to show vulnerability and humility.

We will look at how to build these skills in more detail in Part Two of this book.

2. Personal power

How you hold yourself really matters. As a leader, you must be perceived as having the ability to affect the world around you. Project too much power, and you could be seen as overbearing, dogmatic and potentially toxic. Too little and you will be seen as inconsequential. **Personal power** is about having just enough authority to command people's attention and encourage a belief in you. Charismatic leaders exude confidence and are energetic and positive. They know that confidence is contagious. They are willing to lead and make things happen. They are poised and aware of their body language. They are acutely aware of the signals that they send in their non-verbal communication. They are always dressed appropriately and well turned out. They are determined, and it shows (but they are not stubborn and obstinate). They have high standards and always believe those standards can be achieved. They are optimists. And they are prepared to demonstrate their intelligence, but not flaunt it. Again, these are all skills that can be learned and developed.

To work on your personal power, you need to pay attention to the following behaviours:

1 displaying a *leadership mindset*;

2 being *positive* and optimistic;

3 being *energetic* and passionate;

4 being *assertive*;

5 *looking* and sounding the part.

To have personal power you must be poised – you need to learn to use body language to send signals, you must exude confidence – even when you don't necessarily feel it and speak with the right vocal tones. You must be positive and optimistic – you need to learn how to always see the glass as half-full, and express determination and belief that tough goals can be achieved. This means being a problem-solver – constantly looking for new solutions and ideas to bring improvement and innovation. You must be assertive – you need to be willing to express your views strongly, while learning how to always respect the views of others. You must be energetic – you need to learn to preserve and project energy, without overwhelming others, which means ensuring you get sleep and that you are fit.

You must also be appropriately turned out – and learn what clothes suit you and how your appearance can do good things for you even in the most informal of offices. You must be knowledgeable and learn to be interested in current affairs and big trends, whether they are business or social, in order to know a lot about your industry, your company and the world as it affects you. Mostly, you need to be a leader –always be prepared to step up and make things happen, even if that means doing it yourself.

Personal power is all about how people perceive you. You don't necessarily have to be confident in every circumstance, but you do need to appear confident and encourage confidence in others. You may be tired, but you still need to show bounce if you want others to do the same. You may be worried, but you need to always show calmness and encourage calmness and poise in others. Self-assurance is about believing in yourself, not constantly beating yourself up.

These are skills easy to understand and yes, challenging to implement, but there is no doubt that when you practise the skills you can make significant improvements to how you are perceived. More detail on how to project more personal power is in Part Three.

3. Affective presence (warmth)

How you make the people in your team *feel*, will determine to a much greater degree than almost any other factor, how well they perform. Having an **affective presence** means you can positively influence the emotions of others, by being more emotionally in tune and expressive yourself. You have to win the hearts of followers and make them feel special.

We all have an emotional signature – how we leave people feeling after meeting us. If we want people to be positive about us and, more importantly, what we're trying to achieve, we need to develop the skills that will enable us to have a really positive presence. This means being able to project warmth, being attentive and fully present, displaying compassion and empathy, being appreciative and praiseful, respectful of others, and most important of all, being a really good listener. If you want to have a positive effect on others, you also need to know how to be inclusive, a good facilitator of creative conversations, someone who knows how to build relationships and someone who is truly interested in others.

Everybody wants to feel important, and everybody wants to feel that they're a valued member of a team. You only have to show that you have lost interest by looking at your smartphone, or letting your eyes glaze over, to make people feel that they don't matter. If you don't smile when greeting them, you send powerful signals of coldness and aloofness. If you don't connect with employees on the issues that concern them, you display disinterest, and they are not going to like you very much at all. It is so easy to have a negative presence and too many leaders are completely unaware of the destruction they leave behind them after these sorts of bad encounters.

Making other people feel good is easy with just a little practice. When you are warm and approachable, people are more likely to embrace your ideas. It can be as simple as making eye contact and flashing a smile. It can be as difficult as giving someone your 100 per cent focus, putting yourself in their shoes to truly understand their point of view.

To develop warmth and have an affective presence, leaders need to be:

1 more charming and *engaging*;

2 better, more attentive and *empathetic listeners*;

3 more *respectful*;

4 more *appreciative*; and

5 more *inclusive*.

The irony is that most of us think that charisma is all about being an extrovert. Far from it. It's about making people feel better about themselves after an interaction with you. To do that, you have to learn how to give people your full attention, and not feign interest. With practice, all of these skills become significantly easier. Learning how to have an affective presence is an area where we can quickly make the most significant gains, because most of us are actually unaware of our impact on others. Simply being more mindful about it has a positive impact.

We have to set aside our pride and realize that there is work to be done. For example, I have researched more than 4,000 leaders since 2014, and the vast majority believe that they are very good listeners. On average, they give themselves a mark of 7 out of 10 for listening. Employees rate listening skills as one of the top eight most important skills of a leader, but generally give their bosses a bad rating when it comes to listening. The reason is not to do with whether their boss has comprehended what they had to say, rather it has everything to do with how those employees feel after the encounter, and whether they feel they were truly listened to.

Asked whether they feel that their managers care about them, almost 50 per cent of more than 2,000 employees I have surveyed say no. When it comes to empathy, well over half say that managers don't understand their needs and about 40 per cent feel that their managers don't value their input and perspective. These negative views are easy to change, and with them, engagement and performance.

If you want to start with developing the skills you need to have a more affective presence, go straight to Part Four.

4. Driven by a cause

Charismatic leaders have a cause. You are attracted to them because they are passionate about doing something that matters, something that makes a difference. They have a clear vision of success and they work tirelessly to advance towards it. Their **drive** and energy to succeed are inspiring. They set clear goals, which they are willing to review all the time, and they are open to looking to find ways to improve so that they can achieve their cause more quickly and more efficiently. Their passion for their cause makes them charismatic.

They have learned to talk about their cause in a compelling way. And no matter where they sit in the organizational hierarchy, they are able to connect their cause to that of the organization. They make absolutely sure that their employees are connected as well by making sure they know exactly how they contribute. Charismatic leaders always have their customers at the forefront of their thinking, and it is for them that they want to make a difference. They are in tune with those customers and they make sure that everyone in that team is also in tune.

They are not afraid to set stretching goals and encourage you to believe that you can achieve them. They liberate their followers to take decisions by making sure every member of the team is absolutely clear about what decisions they can and cannot make, and they leave as much as they can to the discretion of team members, confident that everyone in the team is aligned to the cause. That confidence and belief in you is inspiring, especially when a leader ensures a culture in which everyone is enabled to deliver their very best and be collaborative.

To align people to a cause, leaders need to learn how to:

1 develop and articulate a *compelling cause* or purpose, and constantly drive the effort required to achieve it;

2 bring *customers* into every team meeting and decision;

3 align everyone's *goals* to a common vision;

4 deliver *autonomy* through a freedom framework; and

5 develop a deep-rooted culture of *continuous improvement*.

As we will see in Part Seven of the book, neuroscientists and psychologists believe that when people have a clear sense of purpose, a stretching set of goals, and a guiding set of principles, they are likely to achieve more. When people have a sense of purpose, neurochemicals in their brains are released that are more likely to enable success, and these in turn enable positive behaviours that drive progress.

To learn more about how better to deliver a compelling purpose, go to Part Five.

5. *Persuasiveness* ⇨

To be **persuasive**, you have to learn how to connect with others and to communicate with skill. Great communication is not about delivering messages brilliantly. Standing up on a stage and being a great speaker is no good at all if what you have to say doesn't connect with people and persuade them to new beliefs and new behaviours. Being persuasive is about delivering a message that resonates, motivates and engages people. It is all about changing behaviour or encouraging the right behaviours.

When you speak with people in a way that shows them you understand their concerns and issues, when you provide clarity and connection to a cause, when you are able to encourage people to have a conversation, when you understand what it actually takes to change behaviours, only then might you be able to communicate with power.

To be more persuasive, leaders need to learn how to:

1 understand their *audiences* better;

2 facilitate *conversations* and encourage debate on difficult issues;

3 take a stand with a *powerful point of view*;

4 tell *good stories*; and

5 be a *good speaker* on stage.

When leaders communicate well, and encourage their teams to communicate well, employees can innovate at speed, sharing information, successes and failures, and learn to cooperate and not compete. Being an effective communicator is one of the attributes most valued by employees. Good communication has a major impact on whether people feel respected, motivated and more likely to give discretionary effort, yet most employees say that their managers are not visible and do not talk with them frequently enough.

To learn more about how to be more persuasive, go to Part Six.

Integrating skills

Please do not fall into the trap of concentrating on only one of these areas, and not bothering with the other four. Getting slightly better in all of these areas will have a more positive impact than being brilliant at only one of them. It is a combination of these skills that is key to driving up discretionary effort. If you improve your ability to communicate a compelling purpose, if you get better at making employees feel good about themselves and showing them that what they do is important to success, if you improve how you engage with employees and show that you value their input and perspective, and if you have good oratory skills, you can produce a dramatic uplift in discretionary effort for only moderate levels of improvement in each area.

FIGURE 2.1 Charisma traits and skills

AUTHENTIC

INTEGRITY
VALUES
COMMITMENT
SELF-AWARENESS
HUMILITY

POWERFUL

LEADER MINDSET
POSITIVITY
ENERGY
ASSERTIVENESS
LOOK THE PART

WARM

ENGAGING
GOOD LISTENER
RESPECTFUL
APPRECIATIVE
INCLUSIVE

DRIVEN

COMPELLING CAUSE
CUSTOMER FOCUS
ALIGNS GOALS
EMPOWERING
CONTINUOUS IMPROVER

PERSUASIVE

UNDERSTAND AUDIENCES
GOOD CONVERSATIONALIST
POWERFUL POV
GOOD STORYTELLER
EXCELLENT SPEAKER

PART TWO

Authenticity

03

How to be a great manager...
by managing who you are being

Charismatic leaders are crystal-clear about their values, beliefs, convictions and morals, and put them on constant display in the close-quarter combat of daily business.

One of the best leaders I ever worked with was a blunt-speaking engineer from the north of England. He always told people, in no uncertain terms, what he thought. He had the ability to be assertive, while always showing an enormous respect for opposing views. He told people very clearly what he believed, and they could see those beliefs reflected in his daily behaviours.

For example, he believed that efficient meetings required plenty of preparation, and was very tough on people who hadn't bothered. It always became very clear, within minutes of a meeting starting, that he had done his background work and had some ideas already formulating in his mind as to how to solve problems, for every item on the agenda. He always expected the same from others at the meeting and would recognize effort from others even if he disagreed with their views. If, for any reason, he had been unable to review the paperwork, he would admit this and explain why, and then mostly stay silent through the meeting.

He believed in continuous improvement and was firmly of the view that you could only improve if you were open-minded about mistakes, and willing to listen to bad news. I often heard him in town halls around the country admitting to management mistakes, including his own, and promising to take action to fix whatever was causing umbrage or problems. He would then make sure action was taken and make a point of reporting back to the people who had raised the issue. He was especially tough on managers who would cut short the views of others or display closed-minded attitudes.

He would often talk to his beliefs, born of his experiences or his own personal values, and make very clear where he stood on issues. He was visibly committed to the cause, even in the face of vehement opposition. He always showed up and took the flak. His willingness to admit mistakes was a humility that others appreciated. He loved nothing more than hearing good ideas from others and would often respond by saying that he would never have thought of that idea himself. He was courageous about his values and did not fear that others might fundamentally disagree with them. Even if they did, they always knew exactly where he was coming from. Colleagues may not have liked what he was saying, but they trusted his integrity and his sincerity. They never doubted his commitment.

He knew that being a great manager was not only about brilliantly managing what other people did. It was, first and foremost, about managing who **he** was being and what he was doing. He knew that if people didn't trust him, they would resist the huge change programme he was initiating.

He knew that trust was a catalyst for great performance. He often said: 'Trust is money'. He explained that when teams or organizations are highly trusted, everything becomes easier. You can innovate faster. Customers will be more willing to try your new ideas. You can get things done with suppliers and partners quickly and easily. The cost of doing business falls while income rises.

When you are not trusted, however, the cost of doing business escalates. Everything gets harder to do, and suppliers and partners require more diligent contract work. Governments may get involved in policing your every action and impose costly restrictions and controls on what you do and how you do it. Customers are less likely to want to try new products and services, so you have to work harder to get them to buy.

Without trust, a team simply cannot function properly. Everything takes longer, communication becomes more difficult and innovation withers on the vine. Trust and leadership go hand in hand, for very few people are willing to be led by someone they do not trust. If a leader is not trusted, that lack of trust becomes contagious, and members of the team soon start distrusting each other. The contagion can quickly spread in a company and out to customers and other stakeholders, destroying business efficiency and potential.

The trust gap

It is therefore essential that a leader is trusted, gives trust and fosters trust in the team. For leaders to be trusted, they have to be authentic, principled, humble and honest. They also have to be highly visible and visibly committed to every person in the team, to the vision and to the culture of the team. These are all skills which can be practised for maximum effect. To be skilled in all of these areas, however, leaders must be self-aware. Again, this is another skill, which can be developed and honed.

If I was to ask you whether you thought you were honest, whether you behaved with integrity, and whether you had a strong set of principles, I have little doubt that the answer would be yes, of course. I also have little doubt that this is true. The problem comes in inconsistent behaviours, inadvertent hypocrisy, and a simple lack of self-awareness, along with a lack of understanding of your impact on others. It is in these areas that trust breaks down.

While managers say they are honest, a worryingly large number of employees disagree. This is a significant perception gap, and one that points to the need for a lot more work by managers to ensure that they are behaving in ways that deliver a greater sense of honesty, more consistent principles and a greater self-awareness. Being sufficiently self-aware is perhaps the single greatest failing of most managers. When asked whether their bosses understood their weaknesses, only 27 per cent of employees agree. It is bracing, therefore, that only 1 in 10 managers shows any doubts about whether they are self-aware. Bottom line? Almost half of the employees I have surveyed have real doubts about whether their boss is authentic.

To close this gap and be seen as authentic, leaders must be skilled in the following areas:

1 Delivering honesty and integrity, consistently – see Chapter 4.

2 Having and living a personal mission and values – see Chapter 5.

3 Being visibly committed – see Chapter 6.

4 Being self-aware – see Chapter 7.

5 Having humility – see Chapter 8.

As we will see, each of these skills (for they are skills) involves leaders behaving in ways that will be clearly visible to those that they lead. They require you to think about what each behaviour means for your daily routine, and how each and every one of your behaviours might need to change and improve in order to have a positive impact on the people you lead. Let us take each of these in turn and consider what it means for the way you need to think and behave.

04

Authenticity skill 1
Practise honesty and integrity

You are honest and you have integrity. No doubt. That, however, is not the issue. The challenge you have to deal with is how to manage the inconsistencies that make you appear to be dishonest.

Charlotte arrived as the new leader of the business with a big reputation, and her staff were both excited and nervous. Prior to taking up her position as the new managing director of a digital design consultancy, with some 300 employees, she had been a client with a big profile and a track record of sustained success. Charlotte had been a highly demanding client and was now going to be an exceedingly tough boss.

Within two days of arriving and taking up the reins, she was to lead a pitch for a massive piece of business. Her previous experience was both highly relevant to the potential new client and impressive. Although the team tried to involve her as much as possible before the pitch, Charlotte had been heavily engaged in handing over to her replacement at her old company and couldn't give the team any time. She assured the pitch coordinator that she had been on the receiving end of enough pitches to know what good was, and that she would learn her part from the script he gave her and be good enough on the day.

Sadly, she wasn't. The client was more challenging then she had anticipated and less in awe of her reputation than she liked. She wasn't on top of the script, because, while she knew her part very well, she had not bothered to really understand the roles that the rest of the team would play, or fully understand what they were trying to say. She seemed to challenge them just as much as the potential client did. It was clear that she'd not got her head properly in the game. The team left the pitch certain that they had lost, and none too impressed with their new boss.

The next day Charlotte e-mailed every member of the team to apologize for her performance and promised them that she would never again be so lackadaisical in her approach. She had learned a bitter lesson and it would serve her well. She desperately hoped that her performance would not detract from what she believed to be a great performance by the rest of the team. For the next few weeks, she showed great humility as she toured the company and spoke often of what had been for her a humbling experience in the pitch. When the news came that the pitch had, in fact, been won, her joy and relief were touching, and team members were quick to forgive her. Within another few weeks another pitch opportunity arrived, and this time she nailed it.

Honesty wins respect

Charlotte's honesty and humility won her fans in the business in spite of their doubts about her. Had she been arrogant and dismissive, it might have badly and possibly irreversibly undermined her leadership platform. In being self-aware and honest, in showing integrity and putting it on full display for all to see, she bought herself time to earn the respect that she deserved, and when she put her heart and soul into the next pitch opportunity, bringing invaluable experience, ideas and advice to the team, but always with humility and a willingness to learn from them, the team couldn't praise her enough to anyone who would listen.

She displayed a searing honesty and a deep level of integrity. This is something you have consciously to try to do, and you have to practise doing it to become good at displaying it. Without integrity, leaders will soon fail. If, for example, you keep choosing what's convenient over what's right, your team will quickly lose faith. As leaders, we always have to make decisions that, in some ways, define who we are. Without a strong set of values to help guide us, our decision-making will soon become inconsistent at best, and potentially confusing and damaging at worst. In the next section we will deal with how to clarify and articulate your values to enable you to better display your character and decision-making process, but for the moment let's focus on the idea of why we have to 'practise' honesty and integrity daily.

As leaders we are being scrutinized every single moment, and everything we say, everything we do and every decision we make will be picked over by our teams, who will be quick to interpret those actions through their own set of filters. To avoid being thought of as potentially dishonest, or lacking in principles, it becomes necessary to be radically transparent with people – absolutely straight with them about what decisions you're making and why. It is then especially important to ensure there is no gap between your words and actions. This is an area, from my experience, that most leaders are simply unable to see as a weakness. Followers often pay more heed to what you do than what you say.

If you say bullying is unacceptable but do nothing about the super-salesman who is domineering and a bully, the signal you are sending is very different to your words. Followers will take their cue from how you behave, not your words, and the damage is done.

This gap between your actions and your words is potentially one of the most toxic to your leadership effectiveness. Your followers will be watching for consistency – both in your language and in your behaviour. If you even slightly change your story, or treat one member of the team differently to the others, this will send danger signals that you are not to be trusted. You have to be acutely aware of being consistent or explain fully why not when you behave in an inconsistent manner.

I have no doubt that you are honest, sincere and principled. To convince your followers, you need to practise the behaviours that demonstrate your honesty and integrity every day. Without fail.

The following are some potential 'authenticity gaps' to watch out for:

- Employees will judge your integrity based on whether you do what you say you'll do. If you make a promise, deliver it or your integrity will be questioned.

- Ambiguity is your enemy. If you're not crystal-clear about things, people might develop false expectations or misunderstand, and the next time you act they'll think you're being inconsistent simply because they never understood you first time round.

- Defensiveness can be a killer. When people believe that you are closed-minded about a situation, they will hesitate to bring you problems. They will especially avoid you if you tend to go on a counter-attack whenever you are confronted with an issue. You have to practise being open and receptive to problems, even those of your own making.

- Being too egotistical can also lead to people doubting your integrity. If people see you talking up your own achievements, or trying to demonstrate your intelligence too much, they will soon begin to doubt whether you have their best interests at heart. The worst thing you can ever do is take credit for things your staff have done.

- Never, ever lie. Even slight inconsistencies in what you say will be picked up by members of your team but being called out on a lie (or even denying a truth) is fatal to your credibility. If you are challenged on something and are unable or not allowed to respond, for whatever reason, it is always better to simply say that you're not able to talk about that at this stage. Promise to get back to them as soon as you can.

- Think carefully about how you should behave differently, when you expect employees to change what they're doing. These visible signals will encourage change, because employees will be watching you intently to see whether you're prepared to change as well, and only when your behaviours reinforce a new culture, will they believe you.

05

Authenticity skill 2
Have and live a personal mission

*Authenticity is about being true to you, and true to others.
How can you be true to yourself if you are not absolutely clear
about what you believe in?*

Some of the best managers I've ever worked with were inspiring because they were crystal-clear about their beliefs and morals and put those on display in the close-quarter combat of daily business. They were careful to make sure their own values aligned with the stated values of the company they represented. They were then able to be consistent in deploying those values in the workplace. Because they put their values on display, daily and consistently, people never questioned where they stood on issues. They simply knew. This was particularly useful to employees when the boss wasn't around. When facing a problem by themselves, employees simply had to refer to what they thought the boss would do in the same circumstances, what values he or she would apply, and they knew what to do. Because of their values, there was a strong culture in the team, and a strong sense of belonging, because everyone knew what was right and what was wrong, so they all behaved in the same way.

When you have articulated your values, it makes every aspect of your life easier. It helps making difficult decisions easier, and when you live up to your values and beliefs, you always feel happier and more contented. Knowing and living your values is the single most powerful factor in helping you to be more authentic. When you talk about the things you believe in, and then behave accordingly, it makes you more genuine to people, as well as being both emotionally expressive, and more human.

The conviction to prosecute an agenda

Self-belief and conviction are vital to be a good leader. You have to have the conviction of principles to give you conviction about decisions and the conviction to prosecute an agenda that you care deeply about. People can see it, or worse, they can see the lack of it, and that's destructive to trust. Leaders who remain aloof, and don't give of themselves, are difficult to read and always appear to be suspiciously pursuing a different agenda. Nothing erodes trust faster than when employees have suspicions that what you say is not what you believe. They can smell inauthenticity a mile away.

How you communicate your values and your sense of purpose will help people to decide whether to trust you, how much to trust you, and what to trust you about. When you talk about your passion and your values, you provide a framework that powers your conversations with everybody and enables decision-making throughout the whole organization. Authenticity is about being true to you, and true to others. How can you be true to yourself if you don't know who you are? How can you know who you are if you are simply not clear about what you believe in? And if you don't know what you believe in, how can you show people what you're passionate about? To be charismatic and influential you have to learn to show your passion but can't do that without the platform that is a strong set of values.

So, how do you go about establishing what your values truly are? How do you begin to understand the things that motivate you, or the things that are your hot buttons, that make you angry really quickly because of a deep sense of affront?

This is an area I spend a huge amount of time on – helping leaders I coach to unearth and then articulate, in a powerful way, the values they live their lives by. I only really became clear about my own values, and the need for them, when I had already been working for 30 years. Being really clear about my values, my strengths, and my sense of purpose enabled me to pursue a very different journey in my career for the last 15 years of a 45-year journey. It is never too late, and the results can be game-changing.

Uncovering your values and sense of purpose, starts with some intense self-examination, which requires you to make the time to do the work. It is a process, which looks like this:

1 Think about the seminal moments in your career and life, and the key lessons that you have carried forward from them.

2 Understand your strengths.

3 Understand, admit to and mitigate your weaknesses.

4 Define your values and beliefs.

5 Define your purpose.

6 Map your purpose to that of the organization. Take special care to articulate why you believe that purpose really matters. Create a picture of success and speak about it more.

7 Map your values to those of your business.

Let's go through each of these in more detail.

1. Seminal moments

Spend some time thinking about your life from as far back as you can remember. Think about the big things that happened to you that have left a lasting impression. Think about things in your personal life and in your work life. What were these moments? What happened? How did they make you feel? Most importantly, what did you learn from them and how do you behave as a result now? If any of these moments truly did have an impact on the way you behave, try and articulate the belief that now drives the way you behave. This belief is, in fact, a value. I describe a value as a 'belief in action', so anything that drives your behaviours can be thought of as a value.

For example, I grew up in South Africa during the apartheid years. I became a journalist on an English-language newspaper in opposition to the apartheid government. I saw at first hand the dreadful impact of a fundamental lack of respect by one race for another. The contemptuous attitude that they, the white Afrikaner government, were superior to all other races, drove a profound belief in me of the importance of respect. As a result of that experience, I now find myself hugely passionate about the power of respect, and how the world would be a better place if we could all learn to respect each other and each other's views. Every day I practise the art of automatically giving people respect without them having to earn it, and that often pays huge dividends. A hot button for me, one that drives a quick and angry response, is when I feel I am being disrespected or I see someone else being disrespected. What similar experiences have you had in your past?

Before I started work, I had to spend time doing national service in the Army in South Africa. As much as I hated it, I did learn about the power of discipline. Through discipline, I learned that I could do so much more when I applied myself, I could learn new skills and become better, or I could achieve huge projects, one step at a time. This was a revelation to me after being something of a wild child beforehand. This belief in discipline is now one of my values, and has enabled me to write five books, four of them while holding down a full-time job. This belief in the power of discipline translated into behaviours – I am disciplined.

Another example: I am, and always have been, hugely curious. It used to drive my mother mad when I took things apart to try and understand how they worked, and drove her to distraction when I couldn't reassemble them. Much to her credit, however, she only ever encouraged my curiosity and it has been a powerful force in my life that has served me well in so many ways. It is no surprise, therefore, that curiosity is another of my deeply held values and I have no problem at all exhibiting curiosity many times a day, and encouraging it in everyone else.

Those sorts of seminal moments will have shaped you – so what are the key learnings that you have carried forward from them? How have they influenced your behaviour since? We've all had those breakthrough moments in our career when we have had to fight and win in extraordinarily difficult circumstances. In those moments we probably learned things that we have carried forward into our careers and used as a template in many other similar circumstances. Think about the key moments in your career where you experienced either the biggest challenge or the greatest learning. When were those moments? What did you do? What did you learn from this and what do you keep repeating now? Why?

How do these seminal moments define how you behave now and what you believe? Try to list as many of these as you can – we will edit things down a little later. But first, I want to look at your strengths.

2. Understand your strengths

Many of you will already have done some kind of strengths finding exercise, and this can be really helpful at this stage of the values exercise. If not, again you can go online and find a strengths finder website, and do the online test, so we can begin to get an understanding of your strengths. There are many free tests online, as well as ones you have to pay for to get a more comprehensive understanding. It is well worth while, because it is often from your strengths that you can determine your purpose in life.

As well as doing that, ask your friends and trusted colleagues about what they see as your strengths. Sometimes, these will surprise you. They will tell you about strengths you probably don't recognize yourself, and if they're honest they will tell you about weaknesses that you may not want to admit to. I have found that with many of the leaders I work with, they don't recognize their own strengths. The reason is that because when they are working in a strength zone, it simply doesn't feel difficult to them, so they don't see it as a strength. It is only when people who are not gifted in this way point it out to them that they even acknowledge it might be a strength.

Understanding your strengths is useful in two ways – it helps you to be more self-aware but also helps because behind many strengths lie some deep-rooted values. For example, colleagues will often tell me they admire my ability to provide clarity in complex situations. I simply didn't realize that I did this, but the more I thought about it, the more I realized that this came from a profound belief that it was important for me to always fully understand other people and what was going on before trying to make myself understood. Behind the strength was a value. This was to always try to put myself in other people's shoes – this gives perspective and helps understanding and gives you empathy and insight.

Once you've listed your strengths, explore them for an underlying value that drives your behaviours and is the basis of these strengths.

3. Know your weaknesses

The mirror image of knowing your strengths is knowing your weaknesses. This becomes critical when exercising the skill of humility, which we will examine later in this chapter. Examine these weaknesses for any underlying values. For example, it may be that you can't be bothered in certain areas because you simply don't believe in the importance of that behaviour. In looking at your values and beliefs, it is also worth understanding what you don't believe in, and what you don't regard as important. You may well have to re-evaluate some of these beliefs when leading others. Knowing and acknowledging your weaknesses can itself be a huge strength. Being able to admit that you got something wrong is one of the most disarming things a leader can do. Knowing what your weaknesses are and having the courage to speak about them enables you to bring humility to leadership. (And, anyway, those closest to you will already know the truth of what you say).

4. Values and beliefs

Now, ask yourself about the values you believe you live your life by and that are important to you and your family. Think about the values you learned from your parents and their parents. Ask your friends how they see you, and what they believe your operating beliefs are, based on how they see you behaving. List as many of these values as you can. Go online to look at typical values-based words, by simply typing in the words 'values words'. Put down all of those words that resonate with you, and which you could explain to someone else why that word is important to you. Again, don't limit yourself to a small number of beliefs and values here, simply do as many as you can, but do be honest and make sure that these are truly motivating values for you.

Your values inform your thoughts, feelings and actions, whether you are conscious of them or not. When you surface your values and give them the power of clear articulation, they can give you greater consistency, clarity and focus. They help you to understand what is truly important to you. They allow you to be more consistent because, by following them, you will be more consistently you. Spend time thinking about the values that truly drive your behaviours. Write them down. When you have, you can be more consistent, and know more precisely when you aren't delivering them.

By now you should have a lengthy list of seminal moments and the learning you derived from those moments, as well as a long list of values. Looks daunting, doesn't it? Now let's make that list even longer by looking at your purpose.

5. Define your purpose

This, admittedly, is a tough one. Most leaders go their whole lives without articulating their own purpose statement. They spend endless hours discussing the purpose statement of the organization but no time at all on their own. So, ask yourself these searching questions: What do you want to achieve in your career? Why do you exist? What are you here to do? Why does it matter? How does your purpose draw on the things you believe in and your view of the world, or your strengths? These are the questions you should be asking yourself. When you have, write down the answers, and craft them into as powerful and concise a statement as you can. The power of a statement like this gives you a focus, direction and a sense of accountability to yourself about achieving your goals. It can guide your every action.

If you still have difficulty defining your purpose, based on reading through your now huge list of values, strengths, seminal moments, etc, try to see if there is something in them that you could define as a purpose. When I did this exercise myself, one value I wrote down was to 'always be the key'. That might sound strange as a value, but remember I define a value as a belief that drives your behaviour. What I meant by this was that I wanted to be a key that unlocks the leadership potential in others. When I do this, I am in a strength zone, it makes me feel good, and I can make a big difference to others.

For me, this means coaching people, writing books in which I could share what I have learned about leadership, and speaking on as many platforms as I could, to get in front of as many leaders as I could, to help unlock their potential to be even better leaders. This value became my purpose in life. Even when I am with my grandchildren, that value underpins how I interact with them. I'm always asking myself whether I am behaving in a way that will help to unlock the undoubted potential that they have to be wonderful creative human beings.

Perhaps you already know what your purpose is? If so, great. Put it down here. Some of the leaders that I've worked with have said that their purpose is simply 'to make a difference'. At first, I balked at this, thinking it wasn't specific enough. The more I thought about it, the more I realized that the driving need to make a difference or achieve something was what actually makes a leader. They want to make a difference to the people they lead, and the organization they serve, to create a winning team. If there isn't a need for change and improvement, then there is no need for leaders. So, wanting to make a difference is a perfect purpose. What is yours?

6. Map your purpose to that of your team

Whatever your purpose is, find a way to link it directly to the purpose of your organization or your team. Take special care to articulate why you believe that purpose really matters. What benefits do you bring to your team, and what benefits do they bring to those whom they serve? If you do this job brilliantly, what will success look like? Create a picture of success and speak about it more.

Now comes the tricky part. If you are like many of the leaders I have worked with, you might well have a list of over 30 values, all of which may indeed be important to you, but is too many to work with. Now you need to go through this list and think about the 10 to 15 values that are the most important ones to you, and which really do define how you behave every day. This will be the list you work with in your leadership. With each of these values, now try to express what it is you believe about this value, why it is so important. Write down how this belief makes you behave. Now write down how this behaviour has benefited you. You may well find that each of the values has benefited you in different ways at different times. All well and good – these will all be great stories to tell your colleagues to illustrate your values and help you to put who you are and what you believe on full display.

7. Map your values to those of your company

The organization you work for will almost certainly have a set of values that it believes to be important for the culture of all of those who work for it. It will do you no good at all to ignore these values and simply only operate to your own. Firstly, as a manager you will be expected to live the values of the company, and if you don't this will make you seem hypocritical and untrustworthy. However, when you do link your own values directly to values of your company, you can talk to them with greater passion and more insight, because you will care about them more deeply. Where your personal values do not map onto the organization, simply don't talk to them in the workplace. If some of your values run counter to your company's, you will need to think about whether you're in the right place.

When you talk about your values more often you will find it hard not to be passionate. Showing passion is not something you engineer or do in a mechanical way. Talking to what you care about is the trick. When you show passion, it is infectious, and you pass on that passion to others. Passion fuels everything, and when you are passionate about the things you truly care about, you become truly authentic.

06

Authenticity skill 3
Be more visible, and be
visibly committed

*Managers who show up for the difficult conversations
with employees have more credibility and are able to drive
higher levels of engagement.*

The only way you can lead is by being visible, which means being out and about. If you're out and about you will be listening to the people in your business, you'll be listening to customers, and you will be listening to all the people who matter to your team or organization. Leaders have to find ways to make themselves more visible and ensure that everyone in their team or organization hears what they've got to say.

If you lead a small team, it is difficult not to be visible with them, and you probably have little choice. If you lead a national or global team, it gets a little more challenging. You may need to travel a lot and if you do, always walk about the offices and stop and talk to people. Don't make the mistake of attending only the management meeting you travel there for. If you can't get out and about as much as you'd like then make use of videoconferencing, webinars or YouTube, and any other way you can show your face. When you do, make sure you are approachable.

One senior leader I knew spent her life working in what she called 'a man's world' of blue-collar engineers. This, however, never put her off seeing and talking to as many of them as she could. She didn't believe in calling all her managers to come and see her for conferences or meetings, and spent a lot of time planning her diary in order to get out to see them, even if they only worked in small stations of 3 to 5 people. She turned up regularly to have full and frank conversations with everybody, even in the most difficult-to-reach places, on a regular basis. When there, she gave these people her full attention, as if they'd just met in the pub, and would make sure that they not only talked about work, but everyday things as well. She believed there was an art in being real, one of the people, while always maintaining respect.

All too often, I've heard reports from employees who say they almost never see their manager. In one large global manufacturing company I worked with, I recall the CEO doing a survey to find out how often managers spoke with staff. He did this because their most recent engagement survey brought forth hundreds of comments from employees saying that they almost never had face-to-face meetings with their managers, and that most of their communication was via e-mail. The CEO told his managers he would, as a result, be doing a simple audit to look at how frequently they got in front of their employees. Knowing that the audit was coming, managers made sure that they went out to see their team members, several times, before the audit landed. The result was a huge leap in engagement levels among staff, who were highly appreciative of the fact that they were now in more conversations with their leaders.

Visible leadership

In another major organization, going through fundamental change, I gathered a group of managers from throughout the company to work with members of my communication team, to make some recommendations for how we could transform the effectiveness of managers in the organization. They came back with a report entitled 'Visible Leadership', which simply said that if the top team made themselves more visible, more regularly, it would go a long way to helping the rest of the company understand the high-level goals and rationale of the leadership team. More importantly, they also recommended that we had to train up all managers, at all levels, to be better conversationalists, so that they could have the skills and confidence to show up more often in front of their own teams, and hold the critical conversations that were necessary to help people understand why we were changing, and what it was now necessary to do. We implemented the recommendations, and asked managers to meet with their teams more frequently and feed back to us the result of those discussions. This was a form of auditing their actions, because we knew that if we didn't get a report from them about the meeting, it was likely they had not held one. Again, in a short period of time, engagement levels shot up as did morale. Showing up and being visible is one of the most important behaviours of leadership.

When you know the names of your team, and their own personal backgrounds, and you talk about issues outside of work as well as the goals on your mind, you show that you care. When you show you care, you are tapping into the most inspirational thing that a leader can do, which we will cover more in Part Four.

You need also to demonstrate your commitment to delivering the goals that will enable your team to succeed. You need also to demonstrate your commitment to members of your team, asking constantly how you can help them to achieve even greater things.

How can I help?

During 2019, I enjoyed a new programme on Amazon Prime, called *New Amsterdam*. I love TV series about hospitals, and this one is about the new head of a hospital trying to transform its performance and re-engage with its public service mission. In every encounter, he asks doctors, nurses, janitors and back-office staff how he can help them. Every time. It is a great lesson in leadership. By constantly asking his staff how he can help them, he is demonstrating that they matter to him, that he believes in them, and that he cares. Of course, he has to make difficult decisions, which are not always popular, and insist that the team deliver those decisions. He will then make sure that he spends time seeing how he can help them to deliver those new goals.

Being visible truly matters, as does demonstrating your commitment to your own people as well as your commitment to the organization and to success. Often, this may require you to think proactively about how you can behave in new ways in order to send signals to your staff that you are as committed to making changes as you expect them to be.

Modelling the behaviours that you expect of others is extraordinarily powerful but does require some thought and certainly requires commitment. Often, the difference between winning and losing is simply down to the amount of discretionary effort that your employees are willing to give. They only give it if they're committed. If they see a lack of commitment from you, either to the goals or to them as individuals, they will withhold their discretionary effort, and do the bare minimum to satisfy you.

If you are trying to be more visible, it follows that you should also be making sure that any managers who report to you are making the same effort with their own teams. It is always worth remembering that radical transparency is the new norm. Employees have access to websites such as

Glassdoor and will be able to share their opinions about how well they feel their leaders are doing. (Glassdoor offers millions of the latest job listings combined with a growing database of company reviews, CEO approval ratings, salary reports, benefits reviews, office photos and more. Unlike other job sites, all of this information is shared by those who know a company best — the employees.)

It is amazing how often managers hide behind closed doors after implementing difficult decisions. Employees simply think, rightly so, that you're being cowardly. Courageous leaders always show up for the difficult conversations, and sometimes just showing up is the message. Charismatic leaders are always willing to stand up in public for the decisions that they take, even when unpopular.

Additionally, they make it abundantly clear that they are personally accountable for the decisions and actions. If they make promises, they keep them. They make a point of reporting back to people that they have made those promises to. And they are not afraid to make promises in public, if that is what is required.

Ask yourself the following questions about your visibility:

- How often do you show up to have conversations with your employees?
- How visible are you to all of your staff?
- Do you go to see them, or do you ask them to come to see you?
- Do you show up to listen, even if you have nothing new to say?
- When you meet your staff, do you find ways to show your commitment to their success?
- Do you ask people how you can help them to achieve their goals?
- Do you demonstrate your own commitment to your cause? How?
- Do you visibly behave in ways that are consistent with your words?

Make sure people can see what your priorities are by how you spend your time, and where you put your focus. They will be watching. If you say that personal development is important, but never take any development courses yourself, this will be observed. If you say health and safety is an important issue, but never put it on the weekly meeting agenda, this will be noted.

07

Authenticity skill 4
Be more self-aware

Members of your team are highly likely to be marking you down for self-awareness. It is rare that we see ourselves as others do. Who we are, and what we believe and feel, shows up in our unconscious behaviours, and may be sending signals we really don't mean to convey.

Do you regularly ask for and accept constructive feedback? There is often a huge gap between how we believe we are coming over, and how we are being received. Members of your team are highly likely to be marking you down on self-awareness. Time after time, I hear employees saying that their managers simply do not understand their own weaknesses, or the impact that some of their behaviours are having on members of their team. The question is, why is there such a big gap between the perceptions of managers and those of employees, when it comes to whether their bosses are self-aware?

If you're not aware of your weaknesses and people cannot see you strive to overcome those weaknesses, this will undermine your credibility with your team. How you act will reflect in how they act. If being a leader is about managing yourself first, then developing the strength of self-awareness is critical to your leadership success. How can you lead and motivate others by understanding them better, if you don't understand yourself first? Self-awareness is the root of empathy.

Developing self-awareness

Here are some things you can do to develop a greater sense of self-awareness:

1 Take personality and psychometric tests, often.

2 Every day, sit down and reflect and what you have done and why you did it and how it made you feel. Take notes and study those regularly for trends.

3 Ask trusted colleagues and friends to tell you what they see.

4 Ask for feedback, frequently.

5 Understand the stories you tell about yourself.

6 Record yourself, both voice and video.

1. The personality tests

No doubt, as a manager, you have probably already done many personality profiles and psychological tests. If you have, dig these out and try to reflect more deeply on what these are telling you. If you haven't done any of these tests, they are easy to find online. We are all very different, so there are never any right or wrong answers in these tests, but they help us to think about traits we may have or characteristics that we may not fully understand about ourselves. When we have uncovered these traits, both positive and negative, we can demonstrate our self-awareness by talking about them more openly to our colleagues. For example, saying to a colleague that you know that this is a characteristic of yours, but admitting you are not sure of how it impacts on them, will be a powerful signal of self-awareness.

2. Taking time to reflect

Personal reflection means taking the time, every day, to sit down to look at yourself as honestly as you can as a person and a leader. I can hear you saying that you simply don't have the time for this in a brutally busy world. If you want to be a better leader, then this is a powerful exercise. Ask yourself: Why might you be avoiding confronting a situation you are facing? Why are you avoiding doing other things you know might be necessary? Are you stressed, or tired, or feeling demotivated? How might this appear to others? What did you do well today and how did it make you feel? How might that have come over to others? Did you have to compromise any of your values today, and what are you going to do about it tomorrow?

When you ask yourself why you are doing or thinking something, it helps you to clarify your own thinking. That, in turn, enables you to talk about it with others. Being self-aware is not what matters to your employees, though. This may sound perverse given everything I have been saying. But here's the point. What they really mean is: Are you aware of how you are impacting on them?! Are you aware of how the things you do, or the way you express yourself, or the way you do or do not give praise, may be making them feel? They worry about the consequences for themselves, not the consequences for you.

3. How others see you

How do you know how you are affecting others, if you don't ask them? How do know how they feel about policies you have put in place, decisions you have made or actions you have tasked them with? It is powerful to ask people in the workplace how they are feeling about issues. I stress the use of the word 'feeling' rather than the word 'thinking'. If you ask people what they think they will give you an intellectual answer, which may not reveal what's really going on. When you ask them how they are feeling, you invite them to give you their emotional response to issues. Their emotions determine how they behave, and how they behave is exactly what you need to care about.

4. Get feedback

if you want to be able to give people feedback, it seems obvious you should signal that you're prepared to receive feedback. What do you do that sends them powerful signals? What positive things do they read into your behaviours? What do they see that puts them on high alert? What do you do that sends negative signals, in contradiction with what you say? More widely, ask them: What things get in their way in the office? What things do they think we should be doing more of, and why aren't we? What things should we absolutely stop doing, and why don't we? What should we start doing that we haven't tried, and why haven't we tried? You might pick up that they aren't trying things because they are taking cues from the way you behave! How are people feeling about the way things are going? These are all great questions to enable better quality feedback, the answers to which can power better decision-making by you and those above you and help improve performance.

5. *What's your story?*

The stories we tell about ourselves are not just stories – they often define who we are and even shape our personalities. What's your story? How do you tell the story of your life? The better you understand the stories you tell about yourself the better you will understand how they frame how you see the world. Write down the stories you tell about your career and reflect on what they say about you. When you reflect on your day, as I think you should, every day, write down some of the stories about the incidents that happened to you during the day. Examine how you are framing the stories. Test those stories on peers and colleagues that you trust and include close friends and loved ones in that testing circle. How do they hear the stories? What messages do they take out of the stories and the way you tell them? If need be, reframe the stories, to reflect better what you would like people to understand and know about you, or about what needs to be done.

6. *Seeing yourself on video*

There is little quite so bracing as seeing yourself on video, especially with the sound turned off. Ask a colleague or friend to record you when you are rehearsing a presentation, or when you're interacting with another colleague. If you don't want to use someone else's services, use your smartphone. Invest in a small tripod or selfie stick, because I would urge you to do this often and it will be money worth investing. When you have finished, play back the recording and watch and observe your body language, and look for the negative signals you might be sending without being aware of doing so. Try to understand whether you're projecting an open, warm and engaging personality, or whether you come over as closed, aloof, or even inadvertently hostile-looking? Now turn the sound on and turn away from the screen. Listen to your voice and how you say things. Listen to how people respond to you. Try to be kind to yourself and view yourself with a compassionate eye, but nevertheless look for where you can improve.

How you act will reflect in how your team acts. If being a leader is about managing yourself first, then developing the strength of self-awareness is critical to your leadership success.

Here is a checklist to help you gain more self-awareness:

- Do you understand yourself? Are you clear about your strengths, weaknesses or emotional triggers?
- Have you done a few personality and psychometric tests?
- Do you take time to reflect on what you have done and why you did it and how it made you feel?
- Do you ask colleagues and friends to tell you what they see about you?
- Do you ask for feedback, frequently?
- Do you monitor the stories you tell about yourself?
- Are you aware of your body language, and the silent signals you send? Have you observed yourself by recording yourself?

08

Authenticity skill 5
Exercise your humility

Humble leaders are better leaders. Most leaders think that it is damaging to show vulnerability. Contrary to this belief, those who show vulnerability are seen as more human, and therefore as more engaging and effective.

Leadership is not about you; it's about the people you lead, the organization you represent and the customers you serve. When you truly take this on board, you stand a chance of being humbler. Humble leaders are better leaders. These are not leaders who are stricken with self-doubt or are negative about themselves. They simply put others first and fence off their egos from public view. As C S Lewis said: 'Humility is not thinking less of yourself, it is thinking of yourself less.'

True humility allows you to connect with others more easily and leads to engaging them more effectively. When you show that you don't have self-importance, it allows you to show that you think others are more important. You don't spend time trying to impress people with your knowledge or skills or intellect, you let your actions speak for themselves. You give before you get, and you always put others first. Selflessness, however, doesn't mean that you become a doormat.

Charismatic leaders have to stand up for their points of view, but always mindful that other people have a perfect right to a differing point of view. Respecting that point of view is what humility is all about. You're a leader, so you have to make decisions. But are your decisions for your own personal good, or are they for the good of the organization and members of your team?

Humble people are far more likely to admit to mistakes and take responsibility for them, because they recognize that they are just like anyone else, capable of bad judgements or errors. Employees look for fairness in their bosses, which is why humility rates so highly with them. Any boss who cannot admit to their own mistakes, while holding others to task for the ones that they make, will receive harsh judgement.

Charismatic leaders listen more than they speak

Charismatic leaders listen more than they speak and focus on employee needs because they understand that they're not the smartest people in the room. They know that others *will* come up with brilliant ideas if encouraged to speak up, and so they always give others the respect they're entitled to. They always respect differences of opinion and are enthusiastic champions of good ideas, no matter where they originate.

It is paradox that many leaders don't like to be seen as vulnerable or expose their weaknesses, while most employees love it when they do. Being vulnerable has huge appeal, because it shows that those leaders, just like everyone else, have a fear of failure or humiliation but step up to the mark to do things anyway. That courage in the face of vulnerability is compelling.

Only when you let go of your self-importance can you begin to understand how important the members of your team are. As a leader you will never be able to do everything required of you all by yourself, and so everybody else becomes hugely important because it is through them that you get things done. Humility means recognizing those people and giving them credit for what they're doing, especially in public. Taking credit for their achievements is the antithesis of humility.

Leaders who lack humility are terrible to work for. They tend to be more concerned about themselves, and rarely consider the needs of others. In contrast, charismatic leaders are always looking for ways to help their followers and coach them to be marvellous. This is why they generate much higher levels of engagement and performance from their employees.

Have a quiet talk to yourself in front of a mirror. Look yourself in the eyes. Tell yourself that you believe in yourself and that you're allowed to have a quiet confidence. Tell yourself that arrogance is destructive to good leadership. Humility wins friends and followers. Then go out there and demonstrate quiet charisma, by putting other people first.

Here is your 'humility' checklist:

- Do you try to impress others with your knowledge, skills or achievements?
- Are your decisions for the good of the team, or for yourself?
- Do you find it easy to admit your mistakes in public?
- Do you always credit others?
- Do you go out of your way to find things to give others credit for?
- Do accept constructive feedback?
- Do you strive to understand and overcome your weaknesses?
- Are you overtly trying to do something to improve on your weaknesses?
- Do you listen more than you speak?

PART THREE

Personal power

09

How to have a more powerful presence

Employees love leaders who have a quiet confidence and an aura of self-belief and positivity. Leaders who look the part, who have energy and passion, transfer their passion and conviction to their followers.

We all knew the new CEO, because he had long been one of us. As one of the team, Charles had been quiet and unassuming, hugely knowledgeable, and a trusted advisor to the outgoing boss. It came as a surprise to all of us that Charles was now at the helm. We all knew that he had been the CEO of a smaller company in a previous life, but because he had been so quiet as a member of the team, we all felt he was happy not having to lead. Now it became clear that he had been appointed to the management team for exactly this purpose – to be the CEO's successor.

Instantly, his demeanour changed. He seemed a new man. As he stepped into his new role, he stepped out of his shell and stepped into the spotlight with a new charisma. He had a powerful sense of direction, a quiet confidence and a thrumming energy. It was hugely impressive. I must admit that, as a consultant to the leadership team, I was surprised. I had made all the wrong assumptions about him and I now very much stood corrected.

Here was a man I was happy to serve, if he would let me. Suddenly, he had the look and feel of a leader, with a positive mindset and a passion for the task ahead that was magnetic and reassuring. He was a man transformed, and it made me realize that if you want to be a charismatic leader, you need to think, act and look like someone who loves to lead.

Charles did, in fact, make a good leader, and he was a pleasure to serve. He frequently told me that when you took a leadership position, the most important thing to do was adopt a leadership mindset. He said you have to conjure up the personal authority to lead, which comes from being positive, confident, passionate, energetic and assertive. You need to look the part in both dress and body language. You may have the authority that comes with being appointed as a manager, but you will not lead effectively without the personal power that comes from positivity, passion and self-belief.

Defining power

Power is a word you have to use with care in a book like this. Typically, power is viewed with suspicion or given extremely negative overtones, sometimes even evil ones. Power can be used to dominate and destroy people, so I use the concept of personal power here with caveats. By personal power, I mean the strength of character and personality that makes people believe in you and want to follow you. It is a power focused on bringing benefits to the team, the company and to customers. Married to integrity, personal power is magnetic, a force for good.

Leadership is not a position; it is an attitude of mind. It is about choosing to take a lead, and to make something happen. If you are a leader, you see and take responsibility, and change things. Whether people want to follow then becomes a matter of how they see you, which is determined by how you project yourself.

Leaders with a quiet confidence, an aura of self-belief and positivity, give others a sense of certainty, which has a powerful positive effect on their brain chemistry. We like certainty, we hate uncertainty and doubt, so we love leaders who believe that we can achieve the impossible.

We want to see poise and confidence in a leader's body language as well, and we take cues from how managers look and sound. Effective body language can send signals to employees just as successfully as words.

What people wear can affect how they behave, so charismatic leaders also pay attention to their dress, along with their body language and their tone of voice, to make sure the whole picture is aligned.

To work on your personal power, you need to pay attention to the following behaviours:

1 Displaying a leadership mindset – see Chapter 10.
2 Being positive and optimistic – see Chapter 11.
3 Being energetic and passionate – see Chapter 12.

4 Being assertive – see Chapter 13.

5 Looking and sounding the part – see Chapter 14.

You can practise a leadership mindset, just as you can practise positivity. You can take measures to be more energetic and passionate, and project energy to your team. You can learn the skills of respectful assertiveness. You can take measures to be better poised, better dressed and visually more striking. These are all the skills of personal power.

10

Powerful skill 1
Display a leadership mindset

Charismatic leaders have a mindset that says they will be proactive and make things happen, even if it involves conflict and challenge. They seek out trouble and move to the sound of gunfire. They find a way, when others give up.

How do you tackle poverty in some of the poorest countries of the world? What do you do? Give money? Take food? You can, but you won't really be changing much, not for long. If you want lasting change, says Trevor Waldock, CEO of Emerging Leaders, a training NGO, the best thing you can do is empower the poor to solve their own problems... by teaching them leadership skills.

Poor people, says Trevor, tend to be blighted by a poverty mindset, where they simply accept the situation they are in and feel unable to make a difference. They have a hopelessness and lack of ownership of problems that renders them impotent. When you teach them some basic leadership skills, you change their mindset and empower them to write a different story for their lives.

Emerging Leaders has worked for just over 10 years and invested directly in over 50,000 people in 15 countries, with an indirect impact on over 2.5 million people. By teaching leadership skills, they have empowered these people to make a massive difference to their lives. Overall, the people and communities who have benefited from the training report a 161 per cent increase in household savings. About 80 per cent have started income-generating projects, and 65 per cent have set up community projects to benefit their own communities. More than 80 per cent report that their health has improved and 85 per cent report acting to improve their families' education.

A leadership mindset, says Trevor, can be taught. It is about adopting a new mindset and new behaviours by learning new skills. It about lifting your head up and being proactive about problems, taking responsibility to change things and taking accountability for the outcomes. It's about positive thinking: 'I'll find a way' rather than 'I can't do anything about this'. It's about trying different solutions rather than only ever using one solution. It's about keeping on even when the going gets tough.

Adopt the right leadership mindset

It takes leadership to see and take responsibility for what communities want to change, it takes leadership to fight for justice and equality and stand up for the weak and vulnerable. It takes leadership to get more girls into schools or to stop gender-based violence. If people blighted by poverty can face challenges like these and overcome them, then anyone can be a leader.

Trevor Waldock

So, it just takes the right mindset. Leaders who decide to have a positive mindset become more charismatic. Those who seek out problems and move to the sound of gunfire are magnetic. They draw followers to them because of their positivity, their certainty, their bias to action and their willingness to take accountability for their actions. They don't make excuses for a lack of results. They take accountability for everything over which they have even the smallest element of control. No excuses. That means thinking in advance of potential problems and having backup plans. That means considering all options and being ready to take a different course if necessary.

Charismatic leaders make it clear that the only thing they truly control is themselves, and they act as if success or failure is totally within their control. They never blame others, and they never talk about being let down by people they were dependent on. If they succeed, it was down to others. If they fail, it was down to their own failure as a leader. They are certain that there is always a better way to do things. They are always looking for the next challenge to overcome. They have high standards, know that they can be achieved, and expect everyone (including themselves) to attain them. They know that persistence pays dividends.

Certainty has a powerful positive effect on our brains

Charismatic leaders provide certainty, and certainty has a powerful and positive effect on the brains of their followers. A sense of certainty releases positive neurochemicals in the brain, like serotonin and dopamine, and these create positive feelings that encourage people to join in and give of their best. Nothing creates a greater sense of uncertainty than a leader who keeps changing their mind. Indecisiveness, or even an unwillingness to make a decision, is fatal to the confidence of followers.

The Latin word *decidere* literally means to cut off. That's what a decision is – cutting off other options and focusing on a single and final route.

Having made the decision, charismatic leaders paint as vivid a picture of success as they can, every aspect of it – from how it will feel, to who will be impacted, to what benefits will be derived. They convey this picture to every member of the team, so that every individual member can recite it as well as the leaders themselves can, and in as much detail. This creates alignment and a combined sense of certainty and conviction that is hard to resist. The more the leaders recall this picture, the more a conviction of success is hardwired into their followers. This conviction is priceless, and when all things are equal, can make a huge difference.

Once committed to a course of action, charismatic leaders then show resourcefulness. They know how to find and use what is at hand, and how to use those resources to make the best of situations. You can identify a resourceful leader, because they are the ones that others look to in a crisis. They are action-orientated, and they know how to harness what they've got to good effect.

This also means that they not only know that change is inevitable, they see it as necessary, for without change we stagnate. They never waste time trying to hold on to the status quo, they are too busy looking for the opportunities in change, and then trying to align all those they lead. They know there is always a better way, and you can sense that drive they have to improve, do better, make a difference for others.

These are all observable behaviours, which will demonstrate a leadership mindset. Having a leadership mindset will make you charismatic.

Here are the questions you need to ask yourself about your own leadership mindset:

- Do you always look to take a lead, and to make something happen?
- Do you constantly seek out problems and move to the sound of gunfire?
- Do you take accountability for everything over which you have even the smallest element of control?
- Do you often offer excuses for failure? Or do you always take full accountability?
- Do you try to think ahead and anticipate problems?
- Do you look to maximize the resources you have, or get the help you and your team need to succeed?
- Do you constantly strive for a better way to do things?
- Do you set high standards and expect everyone to meet them?
- Do you make decisions and stick to them?
- Do you, for every project, paint a vivid picture of success, and get everyone to be able to recite it perfectly?
- Do you look for the positives in every outcome, but always consider what can be learned and improved next time?

11

Powerful skill 2
Be positive and optimistic

Optimism is charismatic and attractive, an essential ingredient of any significant achievement. Positive leaders reframe challenges wisely and are careful to avoid foolhardiness. However, they don't let fear stop them, and it is sometimes their positivity alone that can make the difference.

How easy is it to achieve something if you don't really believe you can achieve it? How likely is it that you will overcome challenges if you are critical of the team around you? How hard is work when the people around you are negative and defeatist? Impossible, right? On the other hand, one positive person who absolutely believes we can do this thing can make a huge difference to the team, to our mood and to our willingness to even try.

Every great leader that I've had the privilege of working with had what often seemed to me like naive optimism. There were times I felt like that optimism was completely unwarranted, but I then saw how it helped to generate the energy and commitment from the team that was necessary to achieve the results. Just the willingness to act made a difference.

These leaders taught me that optimism without action is simply wishfulness. They knew the odds, and they knew how significant the challenge was that faced us. They also knew that nothing great happened without some element of risk. They were prepared to take those risks and be accountable for failure. Giving something your best shot will not always result in success, but you can derive a lot of positives from trying. The more you learn, the easier it gets next time. Risk-taking is not the same as gambling – which is where you run against the odds in a foolhardy way on an outside chance of success. It is about calculated risks, where there are benefits even from failing.

Charismatic leaders give others confidence

The leaders who demonstrated charisma knew how necessary it was to give other people the confidence that they could achieve the impossible. They knew that positivity drove better performance. They knew that positivity was good for innovation and good for the well-being of every member of the team.

Consider what happens when pessimists dominate the team. Innovation depends on being open to new ways of thinking, lots of alternative ways of doing things, and a willingness to take risks and encourage other people to take risks. It's hard to drown out the voices of those who keep saying 'We've tried this before and it failed', or 'That will never work', or 'That seems really risky'.

Already the negative energy has killed off any impetus to try. It is easy to magnify problems, which often have root in our most basic fears. If you believe a project will flop, it will.

This is not to say that there isn't a role for pessimism, because there are appropriate times when a cautious and risk-avoiding approach is necessary, to avoid the terrible consequences of ill thought-through action.

Optimism requires wisdom

Optimism therefore requires wisdom, and the flexibility to assess situations appropriately. There will be times when a 'can do' attitude is necessary, even in the face of challenges, and there will be times when it is simply unwise to proceed. As Winston Churchill said: 'A pessimist sees the difficulty in every opportunity; and the optimist sees opportunity in every difficulty'. Good leaders practise the art of seeing the opportunity by reframing difficult situations as challenges filled with opportunities.

Optimism is charismatic and attractive, because it is such a crucial part of achievement, especially important when organizations are going through significant change. Optimists are more persistent and do not abandon hope at the first sign of trouble. They also tend to expect the best from others, and that expectation itself can drive better performance.

When you show people that you believe in them, they believe in themselves. When you expect more from people, they expect more from themselves. This phenomenon is called 'the Pygmalion effect', where high expectations of a person have a positive effect on that person's performance. A corollary of the Pygmalion effect is 'the Golem effect', in which low expectations lead to a decrease in performance.

So, how can you develop the skill of optimism and positivity? Do you have to be born with it or can you learn it? I think that even for those of us who don't have it naturally, optimism, like leadership, is an attitude and we can learn it and practise it.

Being more optimistic

1   The first challenge to optimism is our own brain. Our brains look for and focus on threats, which can bring on negativity and its close cousin, pessimism. Try to find ways to beat that negative inner voice and train your brain to focus on the positive. When faced with challenges, always recognize that you will all too naturally identify problems and hurdles… but don't leave them unattended to run away with your imagination. Exercise your self-awareness and understand that your fear centre has been triggered. Instead, ask yourself how you're feeling and try to make crystal-clear why you are feeling that way. What can you identify as a specific aspect of the problem that you can take action on?

2   The next step is to think rationally about the facts, separating those from the fiction that may have been created by your fears. If you don't know all the facts, find them out. (So often at work, I found that problems were a result of mistakes or misunderstandings and not conspiracies, even though my negativity always made me think that people were ganging up on me and trying to find ways to thwart my projects. It was only when I established the facts that I was able to put the conspiracy theories to bed.)

3   It helps if you write down what your fears are – and next to them write down facts to support these, and next to those the actions you can take to solve the problem. The trick here is acknowledging and giving voice to your fears, while then moving on to a more clearheaded frame of mind by concentrating on facts. If you can, identify positives in the situation, and look at the negatives as opportunities to improve. How can you improve

them? As soon as you start thinking about things you can do, you start moving into a more positive frame of mind.

4 Sometimes, you first have to clear your mind and think of anything that is positive in your life, things that you are grateful for. Put yourself in that place and allow the positive feelings to infuse into you. Avoid people who are negative and critical and try to create as positive an environment for yourself. Then return to the challenge. When you then talk to your team about a particular challenge, having done this preparation, you are already in the mindset of positivity because you are already talking about ways that a problem be solved.

This concept of looking for positives in difficulty is called reframing. For example, stop talking about problems as problems. Redefine a problem as a challenge. Simply changing the word reframes the situation, because a challenge can be enlivening and a problem is not.

If someone is being exceptionally difficult, instead of calling them bad names and avoiding them, reframe the issue. Think instead about what might be causing them to behave badly. What emotions are they experiencing, what fears are giving rise to their poor behaviour? Instead of simply accepting a situation, already you've moved into potentially seeking ways to solve the problem.

Instead of seeing a session with a complaining client as a potentially horrendous meeting, see it as an opportunity to better understand their needs and look for other ways to serve them (and make more money).

Reframing takes a lot of practice, but it is an amazingly charismatic skill. When you reframe problems as challenges, you set people on a course of action, and only action can solve a problem. You literally turn them around from fear to positivity.

In a more general way, when there isn't a specific issue or challenge, but you can sense that things are not going well for your team, ask questions that will help you move from an unspecific negative atmosphere to one of more positivity and action focus. What's actually happening? (Facts only please.) Who is involved? Why is it going wrong? What alternatives do we have? And so on.

In these questions you are not only looking for problems, but also the causes and therefore potential remedies.

Positivity and optimism build a platform for creativity. Your team will always respond to it. It's not a question of whether you can solve an issue or come up with a new idea, it's only a question of how. The belief that you can achieve the impossible is not naivety; it's leadership.

To be more conscious of whether you project optimism and positivity, consider the following questions:

- Do you allow your fears to overwhelm you? Are you mindful of being negative and fearful to members of your team?
- Do you consciously project an aura of positivity and optimism, at all times?
- Do you believe that members of your team would say that you do?
- Are you constantly striving to give members of your team confidence?
- Do you practise the 'fear, fact, action' process?
- Do you appropriately acknowledge negative comments and people, but strive to focus on opportunities and action instead? Do you stamp on negativity and criticism if it is out of place?
- Do you try to reframe problems as challenges that can be overcome?
- Do strive to see opportunities in challenges, and articulate clearly what those opportunities are?
- Do you give people confidence by expecting more of them, on the basis that you believe they can perform brilliantly?

12

Powerful skill 3
Be energetic and passionate

Leaders with energy have huge wells of personal power, because they tap into their own passion and consciously convey that passion to all of those who follow them.

You can literally feel when a team has high energy. You walk in the room and the people are buzzing. You know that they feel they can achieve anything, because their enthusiasm is high and their ideas are flowing. On the other hand, you can also feel a team in which apathy reigns. They slouch in their chairs and mope out of the room after the meeting. They are negative about new ideas or change. You just know this team will not succeed.

Energy is power, and leadership is about focusing your own energy so that you can release the energy of the team and achieve your vision. Energy enables action, and passion enables energy. Time and again in the interviews I have done with senior leaders, they have used this word passion, with passion. 'If you don't have passion, go home, for goodness sake, because you will be going nowhere,' said Frank Williams, boss of the Williams F1 racing team, when I interviewed him for my first book.

Most charismatic leaders are inspired by, and inspiring about, the idea that what they do makes a difference, and that what they do is important. This passion is engaging and energizing. Leaders with energy have huge wells of personal power, because they tap into their own passion and consciously convey that passion to all of those who follow them. They know what makes people passionate, and they understand that passion doesn't come from the numbers and targets that we have to achieve.

The language of business is numbers, but for many of us that can be very boring. Action and commitment only follow when people feel uplifted. Too often leaders stay in the world of rational argument, rooting their calls-to-action in numbers. Making a difference, improving your results, satisfying customers, doing good – these are the things that motivate people, not numbers. To be a great leader you have to learn to communicate your passion, because passion begets action. Your passion comes from your values and sense of purpose. It comes from what you care about and your own belief that you, as a leader, absolutely can make a difference and that that is your job. That passion makes you feel fearless and positive, and people find that hugely energizing.

Passion doesn't have to be boisterous

Too often, I've seen people confuse being passionate with being boisterous and 'shouty'. Or they let their anger, resentment or need for revenge fuel a negative passion that repels people. There is such a thing as positive energy and negative energy.

A charismatic leader knows that they not only have to be energetic, they have to *show* energetic. They know that members of the team are always looking at them, always taking signals from how they act. Bosses who are energetic walk and talk with energy. They take care to ensure that they energize themselves, but then they take care to make sure that they are energizing their teams.

Doing an energy audit is a great place to start when working with the team. Simply ask everyone how energetic they feel on a scale of 0 to 10. Why do they feel that way? Is it personal? Or are there things the company does that make it unnecessarily hard and rob people of energy? What do they need to help them get more energized, or stay energized?

Leaders who care about energy care about how much energy their teams have and find ways to energize each and every member of the team. They show that they care about the individuals. They take care not to allow team members to exhaust themselves. They look for ways to help the team recharge their batteries. They always take time to celebrate each and every success, or each and every significant milestone. The watch for when members of the team look apathetic, and, if they do, they seek to find out why and how they can help.

Maintain your own energy levels

Equally, charismatic leaders look to make sure they are able to maintain their own energy levels as well. They find ways to manage their stress. They find ways to ensure they're getting enough sleep. They keep themselves fit. They get up and move about, or take a walk outside in the sun, to re-energize when they need it. (One of my managers used to favour what he called 'moving meetings'. He would always insist on meeting me outside, and going for walk while we discussed whatever was on our agenda. I must admit, I always came back from these walks feeling refreshed and re-energized, often because we had had so many creative thoughts while walking.)

Even as I write this book, I make sure I take frequent breaks. I don't feel guilty about it either, taking my cue from one CEO I work with, who insists that his team never works longer than 45 minutes at a time. He strongly believes that after 45 minutes, a five-minute break can re-energize the room, keep minds clear and focused, and lead to more creative ideas and better decision-making.

Drinking plenty of water is key to energy levels, and clear thinking. I have read a great deal about the need to stay hydrated during a game of golf, which is my passion. The reason is that dehydration kills energy, and leads to poor decision-making, which can ruin a great round of golf in the closing holes. Hydration matters, not just to golfers. Food is energy, so good leaders ensure not only that they are fit, but that they have a good diet that provides the right nutrition to fuel them for their demanding days.

In the knowledge that energy is key to success, charismatic leaders consciously model enthusiasm all time. Even when they feel tired and listless, they fake it to make it clear to the team that energy is required to achieve the goals.

Are you an energy-giving leader or an energy-taking leader? Ask yourself the following questions:

- Do you recognize that energy is critical to success?
- Do you try to be sensitive to the energy level of your team, or of individuals in the team, at all times?
- Do you consciously try to uplift and re-energize members of your team?
- Do you show energy in all that you do, even if tired?
- Do you tap into your passion to energize yourself?
- Do look after your energy levels, consciously and proactively?

13

Powerful skill 4
Be assertive

Assertive leaders leave no doubt in the minds of those around them what they think is important, what they believe needs to happen and why. They may use a strong voice to make their point of view clear, but they never use harsh tones, or hostile phrasing, which can create conflict and turmoil. They are always respectful of others.

People don't respect a leader who doesn't have a point of view. They especially don't respect leaders who won't stand up for the team, or for individuals in the team. After all, real leadership is about taking a stand for what you believe in, or people you believe in. It is about converting people to your cause and getting them to think and act differently in pursuit of your goals.

Not taking a stand leads to a lack of clarity and direction, and that can lead to people being unable to make decisions. It causes ambiguity and paralyses teams. People lose confidence in leaders who are unwilling to make a clear and decisive stand. They will spend all their time trying to second-guess what the leader really wants in those situations.

When you witness a leader taking a stand, with quiet authority, respectful of others but powerfully arguing their point of view, backing it up with passionately held beliefs, the result can be compelling. The result is leadership in action. People will definitely say this person has charisma. This is why assertiveness is a critical skill of leadership. Assertive leaders are able to get their point across without upsetting others, without becoming upset themselves, because they can do so without being aggressive.

When you're being assertive, you express your thoughts, feelings and beliefs in a direct and honest way, always respecting the thoughts, feelings and beliefs of other people. When you're being aggressive, you undermine the rights and self-esteem of the people with whom you're conversing.

No matter how confident and capable, employees can find aggression from their leaders frightening and distressing. Aggression sets off all the wrong brain chemicals and, ultimately, all the wrong behaviours. Antagonistic behaviour puts people down. Where assertiveness is about creating win–win situations, aggression is about creating win–lose situations.

Stand up for your convictions, respectfully

Even passive aggressiveness is detrimental to good leadership, because it results in a failure to communicate thoughts and feelings and, far from providing clarity, makes everything murky and indecipherable. Charismatic leaders create clarity, keep people feeling positive and optimistic, and make sure those people feel valued and respected. Aggressiveness does the exact opposite. Passive aggressiveness and passiveness itself undermine leadership credibility.

Assertive leaders make their points calmly, concisely and coherently. This means they have the courage to stand up for their convictions, set high standards and expect people to achieve them. They are able to give good positive feedback that encourages learning but still makes people feel good about themselves. Assertive leaders are able to say no, to say sorry and to say 'We can!' They always express themselves in a positive way and take personal responsibility for their feelings. They are always, always civil.

Charismatic leaders know that civility is the bedrock of a healthy and thriving organization. They create rules of engagement that foster civility – because civility ensures mutual respect and encourages creativity, well-being and high performance. Sadly, researchers in the United States, who have polled thousands of workers, say that up to 98 per cent of people have reported experiencing uncivil behaviour at work. Christine Porath, Associate Professor at Georgetown University's McDonough School of Business, says that her studies have shown rudeness and disrespect is rampant at work and it is on the rise. She says this behaviour chips away at the bottom line, because people who have experienced incivility respond in negative ways, sometimes retaliating, sometimes passing on their feelings of disrespect to customers or colleagues, but in all cases impairing performance. In a survey

I commissioned from online polling company YouGov, which I outline more fully in Chapter 36, we found that, while 73 per cent of managers said they made the employees feel respected, only 40 per cent of employees agreed.

Encourage civility, at *all* times

To be truly charismatic, leaders need to be seen to be encouraging civility at all times, modelling the right behaviours and encouraging or stopping disrespectful behaviours in the team.

Aggressive leaders all too often will give voice to that aggression in front of other people, and will focus on blame, criticism and sometimes even the humiliation of others. This behaviour creates a culture of fear, a lack of trust, and absolutely kills creativity and risk-taking. Assertive leaders, however, leave no doubt in the minds of those around them what they think is important, what they believe needs to happen and why. They may even use a strong voice to make their point of view clear, but they never use harsh tones, or hostile phrasing which can create conflict and turmoil.

Leaders who are assertive always respect the rights of others but are able to express their views firmly and confidently without putting other people down. They believe in what they have to say and think carefully about how best to express their views, never giving in to angry responses, always behaving appropriately in any heated situation.

Those leaders who have done the work on values that I prescribed in Chapter 5, who have clarified their own values and beliefs, will have a head start in assertiveness, because they will be very clear about the beliefs that motivate the way they behave in life, and will know how to express these beliefs in positive ways. They think about and develop positive points of view.

Assertiveness, like many of the skills of charisma, is not the single key to success, but I will wager that assertive leaders are far more respected than those who are not.

Many managers I speak with confuse self-confidence and assertiveness with dominance, which can be highly destructive to team dynamics. Being assertive, rather than aggressive, and being equipped with powerful points of view, are guaranteed to help you be seen as more charismatic, and therefore more likely to be seen as able to have a powerful effect on the world around you.

Here is your assertiveness checklist:

- Do you always take a stand on issues important to you or your team?
- Do you stand up for members of your team whenever needed?
- Do you always make your views on issues of importance clear to the people around you?
- Do you always treat people with respect when asserting your own point of view?
- Do you ever allow yourself to be openly aggressive or hostile to members of your team?
- Do you avoid difficult conversations?
- Do you ever respond to situations with sarcasm or irony instead of a clear point of view?
- Are you able to say no for yourself or your team, when needed?
- Do you say sorry readily when you are in the wrong?
- Do you encourage and promote civility in your team and from your team?
- Do you think about all the issues of importance to you and your team and articulate clear points of view on these issues before you need them?

14

Powerful skill 5
Look and sound the part

There is no escape from the scrutiny of your team when you are a leader. They watch every roll of your eyes, every scowl, every time you purse your lips, and they interpret the signals without giving you the advantage of correcting what it is that they have 'read'.

Years ago, when I was working at *The Star* newspaper in Johannesburg, I was honoured to know a great South African called Don Mattera, who worked on the paper as a sub-editor. He was not allowed to be a journalist, out and about reporting on issues, because he was a 'banned' individual. The South African government did not like his activist views and had placed him under house arrest and forbade him from putting any of his thinking on public display through his writings, or through giving speeches. With special dispensation he was able to work on *The Star* but only in a backroom role, editing other writers' copy. He is now one of the country's most celebrated authors and poets, and even in his mid-80s is still active in community programmes.

On a daily newspaper, I and many of my colleagues found that writing to a deadline was hugely stressful. After the deadline, when we had all handed in our stories, we would gather around a tea trolley and relieve the stress with jokes and funny stories. Always, hilarity helped to calm us down and get us ready to start all over again for the next deadline. Don Mattera was so often at the centre of that hilarity, because he was a gifted mimic, who was both highly observant and highly imaginative, so his portrayals of his colleagues were always spot on and hilarious, if slightly exaggerated.

On one particular day, however, when Don started to mimic another colleague, I failed to understand who he was portraying. Everybody else was laughing and I assumed that this was someone they all knew that I had not yet met. My inability to identify his target induced even further laughter. Don stood there, jerking his chin upwards and then sideways with his eyes looking towards the ceiling. Painfully, I realized that I was his victim, though I simply couldn't recognize it!

It appeared that I had developed a habit of freeing my beard from my collar with an upwards and sideways jerk of my chin, usually when I was thoughtful and withdrawn. I was completely unaware of this habit, but it was such a visible tic that everyone else could immediately identify me. One colleague told me that whenever I did this, people knew to leave me alone, because I was deep in thought and preoccupied, unlikely to respond well to interruption. Oh, to see yourself as others see you!

No escape from scrutiny

And that is one of the key things to remember as a leader – that people are scrutinizing you all the time, and taking their cues from your body language, probably more than from your words. You might be completely unaware of the signals you're sending. To be a truly charismatic leader, you therefore have to be much more mindful of your body language, and mindful of the body language of others. Non-verbal communication reveals to the world how we feel inside, so it is critical also to achieve emotional mastery if we are to prevent our body from sending signals that may be at odds with the messages we wish to communicate. How you hold your head, where you put your hands, whether you fold your arms – all of these send signals, not only to colleagues but also, sometimes, to yourself.

There is no escape from the scrutiny of your team when you are a leader. They watch every roll of your eyes, every scowl, every time you purse your lips, and they interpret the signals without giving you the advantage of editing what it is that they read. Some of the CEOs I interviewed for my books talked about how they were always conscious of how they walked through the office when passing by their employees. They had learned the hard way that colleagues would be alarmed and worried if they walked through their office with their hands in their pockets and a scowl on their faces. Before long, rumours of closure or job losses would be circulating the entire company, all because they weren't conscious of their body language. One particular CEO told me that she had gone to the length of explaining to all staff that her natural thinking face was a pretty grim face, and they should not take negative signals from it if she appeared to be distracted.

Take control of your body language

Here are some ways in which you can control your body language to become a charismatic leader.

1. Take control of your emotions

The first lesson of body language is to take charge of your emotions, and understand how you are feeling. Your emotional state could well result in a slumped posture, folded arms or a nervous tapping foot. I'd far rather that you consciously tried to assume an open and welcoming posture with your body, to increase the willingness of people to engage with you. If you feel stressed, breathe deeply for 10 minutes. It really works.

When you choose to adopt positive body language, you also send signals to your brain that can help to change your own emotional state. I believe it's entirely possible to change the way we feel and our mood by changing the way we sit or stand. If you're feeling tired, don't allow yourself to slump at your desk, for example. Sitting up straight sends signals to your brain that you still have the energy and discipline to carry on doing what you need to do. Slumping does the opposite. Smiling can do the same thing for you – because it can make you feel happier and it can bring on more of the hormone called serotonin, which is the well-being hormone.

2. A smile is transformative

With the leaders I coach, I often find myself having to remind them to smile more. A smile transforms their faces and is far more engaging and positive. It makes them feel better, and it makes everyone around them feel more at ease. Smiling is contagious. It is amazing how often we forget to smile. A smile is open and trust-inducing, provided you don't smile at inappropriate moments or in an insane way that frightens people. When you smile, try to make it as natural as you can, because a genuine smile produces characteristic wrinkles around your eyes. When you smile only with your mouth, the signal you send is insincerity. A good natural smile, however, directly influences other people's attitudes and how they respond to you.

Always try to look into people's eyes and make that direct contact, even when up on a stage and looking down into an audience. Eye contact is also a positive and trust-inducing signal. Again, though, too much eye contact can be disturbing, so it's all about getting the balance right.

People love being listened to and heard, so another positive body signal is to lean in and cock your head slightly when listening to a member of your team. Nod often, but not too vigorously, as this may be taken as a signal of agitation. Try to be open in your posture, and be conscious of folding your arms, or putting your hands behind your head (a sign of arrogance, but also a gesture that may reveal sweaty armpits).

3. Talk with your hands, but not aggressively

Talk with your hands and allow them to be as expressive as you are, but watch out for aggressive hand signals, such as chopping motions or finger-pointing at people. Watch out for 'hidden hands', either behind your back or in your pockets. Watch your feet, as well, as crossed feet or vigorously tapping feet also send negative signals. Try not to be fidgety, as this displays agitation. An expressive face, with still hands and feet, display poise and engagement. And don't forget the power of a good warm handshake, as opposed to the dominant action of a hand-pumping, too-tight handshake.

Be conscious of space. It is good for a leader to take up as much space as you can, displaying confidence and that you are comfortable, but don't invade the space of others, and stay aware of their space boundaries. Always try to include people when standing in a group, and don't exclude people by standing with your back to any of them.

Be conscious of your voice as well and use your voice deliberately. Too high-pitched and you sound hysterical. Well-modulated and deep, from the chest, is good. Pacing matters as well and speaking too fast is often a sign of nervousness, especially when you're up on stage. (Speaking too fast can also make you breathless, which will only worsen your nervousness, and even cause your voice to tremble for want of sufficient oxygen.)

Think also about gently trying to mirror the body language of people you're with, not making this too obvious and especially not if the other person is angry or defensive. When you do mirror the body language of a member of your team, you set them at ease and send powerful signals of engagement.

Always remember that a huge part of the conversation is taking place in the faces and bodies of the people you're dealing with, so you need to be conscious of their body language as well. Are they making eye contact with you? Are they closing themselves off from you?

4. Send signals with your clothes

Be aware, also, that you send signals by the way you dress and by the way you groom yourself. Poker players, for example, will watch whether an opponent is sloppy with their chips, because that may well indicate sloppy thinking in the game. Sloppy dress will send a signal, so always dress with care. You might be in an office that still prefers formal and smart dress, or you might be in one that is casual and informal. It doesn't matter, but the care you take in the way you dress will. If you show from the way you dress that you don't care, this will send signals that you really don't want your staff reading.

I remember one leader telling me how his wife started buying him long-sleeve shirts with a double cuff. He noticed within a week or two that many of his staff were starting to wear the same double-cuff shirts. Until that moment, he had not been aware of how members of his team were taking cues from how he dressed. Other leaders told me how they paid particular attention to whether members of their team bothered with clean shoes, with clean fingernails and clean hair, and that job applicants who did not pay attention to these small details were quickly sent packing.

Finally, learn from my humiliating experience on *The Star* newspaper, when I was completely unaware that I was being mimicked. Ask your colleagues and members of your team what signals they pick up from your body language. Ask about nervous tics that you have that they are aware of, and what they read from them. Ask them to help you rehearse your body language when making presentations. If you don't have anyone handy, film yourself on your smartphone, and when you play back the video, turn the sound off to watch what signals you are sending. You're likely to be surprised, even when you think you're on top of what you're trying to get your body to say. Charismatic leaders understand that they can build their own brands, build trust and build relationships with better body language.

Your facial expression and body language can reinforce or undermine everything you have to say: be aware of this and make it work for you. Remember that charismatic leaders clearly love what they're doing and show it in everything they do, and in every expression. As a result, they are hugely infectious. They communicate positivity and optimism and they do it through smiles, by walking with energy or by standing straight and tall.

Are you using your body language to best *effect*? Ask yourself:

- Do you remind yourself, often, that you are sending signals through your body language and appearance?
- Do you consciously use your body to send signals to yourself and master your own emotions?
- Do you smile often enough?
- Do you make sufficient eye contact?
- Are you conscious of sending signals of agitation or impatience through your hands and feet?
- Even when not directly engaging with your staff, are you always conscious that they will be watching your every move for signals?
- Do you watch the body language of members of your team to stay tuned to how they may be feeling?

PART FOUR
Warmth

15

How you make people feel determines how they perform

Every leader has a distinctive emotional signature, which they imprint on every person they meet. That emotional signature is one of the most powerful tools of motivation. How you make other people feel will determine how motivated they are, and that will determine how well your team performs.

The first half-hour of Lois's day is a joy to watch. As managing director of a 60-person agency, she loves to walk around her office chatting to staff before the day gets underway. She is a manager I coached, so I know that she instructs her secretary to ensure that she has no formal appointments before 9.00 am. She always gets in around 8.15am to walk around and chat with her early-starter staff. She asks them how things are going, how they are feeling and really listens to what they have to say. She knows their names and the names of their spouses and children. She knows what issues they're trying to cope with both at work and at home. She asks how she can help, or what they might need in order to better deal with the challenges. If they have any specific queries or requests, she makes a note and promises to get back to them. She compliments them on work done and is always looking for ways to connect one member of staff with another. As people come into the office, she greets them and chats with them in turn.

By the time she returns to her own desk, nearly everybody in the office is smiling. They have been warmed by her presence, visibly touched by her attention, and positively affected by her engaging personality. To watch her work the office is to watch a pro, because Lois hasn't always been this way. She is a deeply thoughtful person, and unless she pays careful attention to her own tendencies, she can be very withdrawn and insular, lost in her thoughts. She has learned to be warm and charming, and practised it so much that it now seems natural. She doesn't have a lot to say herself and spends a great deal more time listening than talking. She doesn't make many jokes, but often joyfully laughs at what others have to say. These walkabouts are not about her, she makes it all about them. She has totally bought into the idea that the single most important thing a leader can do is make other people feel valuable, respected and part of something bigger than themselves, so she devotes a lot of time and effort to doing exactly that.

Think about your impact on others

How do you think *you* make other people feel? Do you make them feel nervous? Do you make them feel anxious? Do you inspire them? Do you frustrate people? Do you bore people? Have you even stopped to think about your impact on others? It is highly likely that you don't know for sure how you affect others.

Next time you are in the office, look around the room and pick someone. How does that person make *you* feel? Try someone else in the room, or imagine a colleague or boss. How does that person make you feel? There will be some people you love to be with and who always leave you feeling better than before you engaged with them. There will be others who leave you feeling frustrated and annoyed. Each and every person has an emotional signature, which if you stop to think about it, is distinctive. After being with them, you'll leave feeling their unique touch, whether it's positive or negative. They will have left their emotional signature on you.

Sadly, too few leaders think about paying as much attention to their emotional signature as they do to their written signature. Yet, as a leader, your emotional signature is one of your most powerful tools to motivate others. How you make other people feel will determine how motivated they are, and that will determine how well your team performs. In fact, there is no other management behaviour that matters more to employees. Leaders who make their people feel respected, valued, trusted, and part of a team with shared goals, will always have better performing teams. They are effective because they are affective.

Be *affective* to be *effective*

We sometimes confuse the words affective and effective, even though they have very different meanings. The word 'affective' describes something that has been influenced by emotions, is a result of emotions, or expresses emotion. The word 'effective' describes something that produces a desired result.

As a leader, you have to be affective in order to be effective. How you make members of your team feel will absolutely have an impact on how they perform. You have to be conscious of this no matter how you personally feel. Charismatic leaders are brilliant at self-monitoring in order to exercise emotional control. They're the ones who leave us feeling warm even if they're feeling sad. They know that it's more about how they leave others feeling than it is about how they themselves feel, so they develop the skills that enable them to have a positive affective presence. Equally, poor managers will be unmindful of how emotions are contagious, and they will not care about how their own emotional state impacts on others. They will have a consistently negative affective presence.

To develop the skill of warmth, leaders need to work on the abilities that will make them more engaging, attentive, appreciative, inclusive and respectful. If you are engaging and warm, you will attract people and easily set them at ease, quickly able to make them comfortable in your presence. By being attentive, and applying the skills of listening and empathy, you can demonstrate that they are important to you, and that you care about what they have to say. By learning to be more appreciative, you can give people the respect they earn through their good work or good behaviour. By being more respectful, you are able to give them the respect they deserve and expect as another human being. When you are more inclusive, you bring people into the team, make them feel they belong, and build powerful relationships and a strong culture. When people feel worthy, appreciated and respected, when they feel part of a team, and that their ideas and insights are valued, their levels of personal motivation skyrocket.

To develop warmth and have an *affective* presence, leaders need to be:

1 More engaging – see Chapter 16.

2 Better, more attentive and empathetic listeners – see Chapter 17.

3 More respectful – see Chapter 18.

4 More appreciative – see Chapter 19.

5 More inclusive – see Chapter 20.

Being a good listener is regarded by employees as one of the most important skills of a leader, but most employees rate their bosses poorly for their listening skills. Conversely, leaders tend to rate themselves highly. Also, most employees say they very seldom get the appreciation they deserve for good work, and that their managers seem to find it difficult to give them praise. Worse, many say that they are often disrespected at work, leaving them feeling angry and demotivated. These issues are all easy to fix if managers are simply more mindful of what is needed and more practised at delivering it.

16

Warmth skill 1
Be more engaging

To be more engaging as a leader, you have to be present, focused on people and interested in them. Charismatic people are happy to see you, and when they look like they are enjoying themselves in your company, that positive feeling is contagious and uplifting.

The most engaging people I know are the ones who are more interested in me than I am in them. I see them approach me and I can see from their smiling faces that they want to get to know me, or that they're happy to see me again. They send a signal that I'm interesting. I can't help but be engaged.

Like all of the skills in this book, this does not require a complete transformation of your personality, but it is about being more mindful and willing to practise new behaviours. Being engaging starts with your attitude, which starts before you even meet anybody.

You have to start by setting your mind the right way. Tell yourself that you're interested in them and that you want to get to know them. Tell yourself that everyone has something of value to tell you or teach you. Your job is to find out what that is. To do so you have to be present, focused on people and interested in them. Tell yourself you are glad to see them, because you're interested in what they've got to say. Do that, and it shows. It shows in your body language, it shows in your smile, and it shows in your handshake and attitude. If you don't want to be there, and you don't do something about your attitude, it's going to show.

Think of your employees as guests

Instead, think of everybody as being a guest in your house. Are you thoughtful about their needs? If you think of them as a guest, rather than an interloper, it shows in your face. If you think 'guest' rather than 'difficult person', you will radiate warmth. When you do, you make an immediate impression on the people around you. We all know that people judge us within the first few seconds, whether we are meeting them for the first time or the thousandth time, and they're summing us up through all the visual cues that we give them. We've all had difficult people on our teams, and it is with them that we have to work hardest to be charming. It is so easy to let our displeasure or annoyance show. And that will simply make the difficult person even more difficult.

If you think of yourself as a host, then civility is the name of the game. You try to anticipate their needs to show them that you are thinking about them. You might say something like this: 'I was thinking about the presentation you going to give tomorrow, and thought you might find this article interesting.' Always consider the other person – I hate it when people interrupt my work and show little consideration for what I'm trying to do. I'm always charmed when the person on the other end of the phone asks whether I have two minutes to help them with an issue, or would it be better if they called me back? It shows they respect me and my time. It shows they are polite and civil, and I am far more likely to be accommodating.

Charismatic leaders try to be approachable. They look happy to see their staff, and they treat them as equals. They go out of their way to make employees feel important, and if they're meeting someone for the first time, they convey that they are excited to get to know them. They expect to be pleased and it shows. They always look for the good in team members and look for the strengths in them, and therefore are more likely to find them. When they are greeting a team member that they've seen every day for the last five years, charismatic leaders show they're really interested in how the team is feeling and what they're doing. However, leaders who start with some malicious gossip or some critical comments about their surroundings will definitely convey a lack of charm. This is so easy to do, because we are likely to notice things that annoy us or make us ill at ease in any strange environment – we are wired to do it – so we have to work hard look for the positive.

It all comes back to attitude. 'I will be present and interested,' you tell yourself, and you are. When you think of being warm, it is self-fulfilling. If you act warm, even when you don't feel like it, you become warm. If you act interested in people, and ask them interesting questions, you will soon actually be interested. This is the essence of being engaging and charming. Even as you approach people, try to scan their body language to sense what frame of mind they are in. You might be able to use what you sense to open up the conversation. Try to tune into them even before you say a single word.

If you are meeting people for the first time, once you've introduced yourself, and they tell you their name, try to use their name as quickly as you can and then as often as you can. I try to do this because I know I'm terrible at remembering names. It's not always easy, especially when there are several people around, so I find myself quite openly saying to people that I'm so sorry but I've forgotten their name and please will they repeat it for me. The very fact that I want to remember their name enables them to forgive me and repeat it, which I'm much more likely to remember second time around. If you're meeting one of your team members, greet them by name. It really matters, because we love to be recognized, and our names are a huge part of that.

Use their name and pay a compliment

Having used a person's name, now try to find a way to immediately pay that person a compliment or express appreciation. 'I've been thinking about that piece of work you've done, and I have to say I was so impressed because that has really jumpstarted our sales efforts.' A compliment must be specific to have impact, and even with strangers, can be used to start a conversation. 'I really like your handbag, where did you get it? I might be able to get one for my wife.' You can't be too personal to a stranger, but complimenting him or her about an item of clothing or an accessory is actually complimenting their taste, and will get you off on the right foot. It shows you've noticed them or something about them, which means you're paying attention. (If you are on the receiving end of a compliment, always be gracious, rather than dismissive.) If you can't think of a compliment, then express how glad you are to have them there or to meet them. Or say you've heard really good things about them. Anything to warm them to you.

Show some vulnerability, that's really charming. It's emotionally challenging, but charming and likeable people aren't afraid to open up. Charismatic leaders don't need approval from others, so they don't need to appear to be perfect. (In fact, they are well aware of the fact that perfect people are far less likeable.) Ask for help in some way – ask the way to the bar, or the cloakroom. Ask if they know the format of the evening and what's likely to happen next. With a member of your team, find a way to show your foibles and vulnerabilities. Tell them you need their help in something important. Employees are always more drawn to leaders who show vulnerability and humility.

Always truly focus on people and give good eye contact. People will quickly decipher feigned interest so, to convey interest and presence, you must actually be present. If your eyes are flitting around the room, you send powerful signals of shallow interest. Use kind eyes. You know that feeling you get in your eyes when you look at a loved one with kindness? I'm sure you do. Use that look – eyes are windows to the soul, so if your soul couldn't care less, others will see it. You can help yourself with a little half-smile, but make it genuine, because only genuine smiles put those little wrinkles around our eyes that relax them and make them look like 'kind eyes'. Put warmth in your voice, and invite them into a conversation. Communicate kindness and warmth with a softer tone, heated by a smile. This works especially well on the telephone, when people cannot see you.

People who look happy and look like they are enjoying themselves are naturally charismatic. They have a joy of life that shows through and is hugely attractive. When they show pleasure in their experiences, or in what team members are telling them, it's hard not to infect others with the positive experience they seem to be having.

Those first few seconds of meeting someone count for a lot, whether you are meeting for the first time or the millionth time. Always try to leave them with your positive emotional signature, even if you don't stop for a long chat.

Here's the checklist:

- Do you recognize that you have an emotional signature? Are you always conscious of how you leave other people feeling?

- Do you try to be warm with people? Do you smile, do you open up to them, do you consciously show them through your posture that you are interested in what they have to say?

- Do you 'tune' your attitude to 'positive' before meeting new people, or engaging with your staff?

- Do try to imagine yourself as a 'host' in every situation – mindful of the needs and feelings of your 'guests'.

- Do you look for things to compliment people on when you see them?

- Do you strive to remember and use people's names?

- Do you try to make sure that you look happy to meet new people, or see members of your team?

- Are you prepared to be vulnerable, or ask for help?

17

Warmth skill 2
Be a better, more attentive and empathetic listener

Sometimes, the act of listening is inspirational in itself. Listening leaders make employees feel valued and heard, a key factor in motivation levels. No leader can be warm and affective without being a good listener. But good listening isn't just about understanding what's being said...

Charismatic leaders are intent on connecting with people and giving them the gift of their undivided attention. It is a skill, for we all have to work hard to overcome our natural inclinations, which make us bad listeners. We get easily distracted. We want to have our say, so we interrupt. If we don't interrupt, we concentrate on what *we* want to say and wait for a gap, rather than focusing on what's being said. We get impatient. We make judgements about the speaker, which blocks our ability to hear what they're really trying to say. We become narcissists and speak more than others; we get angry when we hear things we don't like.

Perhaps we do listen, but we become more interested in content than in feelings. We don't try to observe body language, so we stare into space while listening. Or perhaps we listen without any facial expressions, remaining silent throughout. Then we leap in with solutions and don't bother to show that we have comprehended what we have been told. We certainly don't acknowledge how the other person might be feeling as a result of what they are describing to us.

We've all been in the situation where we feel that the person we're with is not really listening to us, and isn't very interested in what we have to say. They leave a powerful emotional impact, and it isn't positive. If that person is our boss, and we go away frustrated and belittled, our motivation level and sense of engagement are going to drop, dramatically. Our feelings of responsibility, control and importance have taken a heavy hit. As a result, we will do the bare minimum, rather than give our all. In the gap between doing only what we have to do and going the extra mile lies the difference between acceptable and exceptional performance. It's in that gap that charismatic leadership pays dividends.

Sometimes the simple act of listening is inspirational in itself. By listening, leaders can remove barriers, pick up good ideas, create goodwill and create an environment where people can speak up without fear of repercussions. They feel connected. They feel valued. They feel that they've been listened to. You may not agree with them, but if they feel you've really understood them, they'll be more likely to listen to why you're not going to act on what they've suggested. By listening to them and showing them that you respect their views and understand their point of view, even though you disagree, you earn the right to be heard.

The listening contract

This is what I call the listening contract: first I have to listen and understand, before I can speak and be understood. It is when leaders do not follow this contract that they create ill feeling among employees. Most leaders rate themselves highly for listening skills, while their employees inevitably rate them poorly. Why is that? The answer is all about whether the employee feels that they have been listened to. It isn't about whether the leader has comprehended what they have to say, which is how most leaders judge their listening skills. Most leaders are smart people, which is why they are in a leadership position.

This is why they will often quickly and correctly understand what is being told to them. So, they interrupt. They provide solutions, not coaching. They do not judge themselves on whether they have made the speaker feel like they have been given a damn good listening to. Yet, that's exactly what the employee wants. So, the first thing to do, in order to become a better listener, is to understand that employees want to feel as if they've been listened to and that their views have been heard and respected.

To do this, charismatic people connect empathetically. Why? Because they know that empathy is the glue that holds relationships together. Empathy enables you to know whether you have managed to influence the people you need to influence. It enables you to understand their perspectives and how to deal with them. Without empathy you can't build a team, you can't build trust and you can't make people feel validated.

To be empathetic means to be able to detect the other person's emotions and understand their perspective. You can't be a good listener if you lack empathy. Being empathetic promotes trust and that leads to open and honest communication, and that leads to the ability to resolve conflicts, to promote constructive change and to innovate.

Leaders who are empathetic go beyond simply trying to understand others and their feelings; they are moved to take action and to help however they can. They show both positive and negative empathy. They show that they are thrilled for others when they do a great job, or get a promotion or gain a qualification. They comfort others when they experience difficulties, at work or at home. They support people when they sense that they are facing challenges, which threaten to overwhelm them.

Empathy is about listening beyond the words and into the heart of the speaker. How are they feeling? Why are they reacting this way? What must it feel like to be in their shoes? Empathizing doesn't mean agreeing. Empathizing is about relating to someone. It is about setting aside your own view of things to fully understand the other person's. Always try to understand what's behind a colleague's new idea, before dismissing it as a dumb idea. There may be value in their motivations if not in the suggested actions.

The direct link between empathy and commercial success

There is a direct link between empathy and commercial success. Leaders who treat their staff well do so because they are tuned in to their needs, and respond in appropriate ways. Being a good listener means paying attention actively. You have to remember that listening is not about you, so you have to focus on what's being said. Stop worrying about what you're going to say. Set aside distractions, including smartphones, and put the speaker at ease by looking interested in what they have to say.

Remember that judging someone is not listening, and as soon as you show that you're judging, you will ruin your attempt to listen. Patience is everything. Show that you're listening by nodding, smiling and using other facial expressions. Watch for signals in the speaker's body language, which will be sending you as many messages as the words they are using. Lean forward, nod often and recognize that your face will be sending signals back to the speaker. Take notes, because that sends a signal that what you're hearing is important.

Show that you recognize the emotion behind what they are saying. 'I can see you're excited about this idea.' Or 'I can see you are upset about what happened.' Relate to them by expressing how you might feel if you were in their shoes. If you are not clear on the emotion behind the sentiment, ask: 'How did you feel about that?' Try to ask open-ended questions, or questions to clarify. Good listening is a two-way process, and the more you encourage people to speak, the more you will glean from what they have to say. Ask questions that further discovery and enable better insight. Reflect back to them what you have heard but avoid parroting back exactly what they've said. This gives them a chance to agree, expand or refute your understanding.

Remember that empathetic listening is all about showing people that you have understood not only the idea or issue they are raising, but the emotional content behind it as well. Always summarize what you have understood and thank people for taking the time to share with you. As a leader your job is to build relationships and trust, so when you thank them for speaking, even if you don't think there is value in what they have to say, you will make them feel respected and valued – and that's the point.

Finally, always commit to action. Make a note to follow up and explain what you have or haven't done as a result of the conversation. People will always feel more committed and engaged when they believe that you will think about or act on what they've said. There will be times when you need to go back to them and explain why you haven't acted on what they've said – it's cowardly not to do so – and this will further build trust and respect.

There will be times when you have to nudge and steer the speaker to see the issue in a different light. This will require thoughtful questions that encourage them to think differently, or skilful suggestions that open up alternative ways of thinking. Once you've fully understood what they have to say, you can now challenge or disagree, encouraging them to feed back to you what they understand from what you've said. We often think that communication is all about standing up and telling people what they need to know. The big mistake is to assume that they've understood what we mean. Skilful communicators always check what has been understood as part of the process of communicating.

Poor listening cuts a leader adrift

Poor listening is destructive to team dynamics and cuts a leader off from the information they need to truly understand what's going on and manage the business effectively. This is why it is essential that leaders understand how toxic it is when they display displeasure at bad news. Do that, and it's likely you'll never get bad news from that individual again. Change your mindset and be a bad news junkie. Show people how much you want to get bad news. The faster it gets to you the faster you can take action.

Good listening isn't only about one-on-one listening. It's about encouraging members of the team to be good listeners. It's about listening to customers, listening to colleagues and, especially, listening to your team. It doesn't matter whether you're an introvert or extrovert; either way you will still have to work on your listening skills. Introverts tend to listen well but don't share their own views as much during a conversation. Extroverts like to share their views too much and need to work hard to ensure they don't dominate the conversation.

No leader can be affective without listening. Listening is part of the process of decision-making, of developing and maintaining relationships, of problem-solving, of influencing, of driving change and of so many other aspects of leadership. Good listeners hear the speaker's words, understand the messages and their importance to the speaker, and communicate that understanding to the speaker. Good listeners are charismatic, because they make people feel important and valued.

Here's the good listener's checklist:

- Do people tell you that you are a good listener? If not, why not? If you don't know, ask them!
- When listening, do you:
  - interrupt?
  - get distracted?
  - listen with half your attention?
  - think about what you want to say and wait for the chance to say it?
  - get impatient and show it?
  - stare into space?
  - have an impassive face?
  - fail to observe body language?
  - fail to listen for the emotions behind what is being said?
- Do you try to ensure people feel that you've given them a good listening to?
- Do you listen with empathy? Do you show both positive and negative empathy?
- Do you summarize what you've heard?
- Do you act on what you've heard, and then tell people what you've done?
- If you haven't acted, do you explain to people why not?
- Do you encourage all around you to be good listeners?
- Are you a bad news junkie?

18

Warmth skill 3
Be more respectful

Uncivil behaviour chips away at the bottom line, because it has a knock-on effect that goes all the way from employee to customers and beyond. Charismatic leaders manage their anger and do their utmost to curb provocative behaviours, always showing respect to everyone they meet.

Everybody wants to be respected. We want two kinds of respect. We want to be respected as human beings, and we want to be respected for our achievements. The first kind of respect is owed to everybody, and should be given freely to everyone, equally. The second form of respect is earned, when people perform well or behave in valuable ways. These positive behaviours deserve to be recognized, frequently. Sadly, employees feel that their bosses do not give either type of respect enough.

The result is highly demotivated people, who feel that their bosses treat them unfairly, and fail to recognize effort when it is given. Nothing is more demotivating, and more likely to cause disengagement and poor performance. A lack of respect can have devastating consequences.

A specialist in the area of civility is Christine Porath, Associate Professor at Georgetown University's McDonough School of Business in the United States. She is of the view that rudeness and disrespect are rampant at work and, in spite of an age of heightened political awareness, is actually on the rise.

She has polled thousands of workers about how they are treated on the job and says that few organizations recognize the issue and take action to curtail it. Respectfulness is regarded as the most important attribute in a manager. My own research, outlined more fully in Chapter 36, shows that while more than 70 per cent of managers feel they do respect their employees at work, less than 40 per cent of employees would agree. If managers could improve their performance here, they could reap a massive payback – a huge leap in discretionary effort.

Never fail to be respectful: encourage respect

Charismatic leaders never fail to respect their colleagues. They always lead by example. This means that they not only never treat other people with disrespect themselves, they never allow anyone else to either. They stamp on incivility when they see it. They foster mutual respect and courtesy.

They lead by example, and unfailingly treat people with courtesy, politeness and kindness. Even when they do have to discipline a member of the team, they do it in private, and with respect.

They encourage diversity and are at pains to ensure that diversity is not only seen as an issue of race, gender or religion, but also embraces different working styles, personalities and generational attitudes. They know that genuine diversity leads to more agile teams, because it brings different ways of thinking together and unearths a greater variety of ideas, perspectives and skills.

They do, however, recognize that diverse teams can easily lead to people not always seeing eye to eye, and lead to more disagreements, so they are always ready to step in and ensure that every member of the team is respectful, professional and even pleasant at work. Charismatic managers ensure that no one is disregarded; no one degrades another colleague, and no one makes another member of the team feel unworthy or unwanted.

Do you take care to manage your anger, or annoyance at work? Do you try to prevent angry outbursts, and curb provocative behaviours?

The benefits of respect in the workplace are enormous – civility leads to reduced stress, conflicts and problems in the team, because it leads to better communication and collaboration. That in turn leads to increased productivity, more agility and increased rates of innovation.

Respect contributes to job satisfaction, and also to employee engagement. It helps employees feel safe, trusted and willing to exert themselves in support of the cause. Charismatic leaders never show disrespect, to anyone.

Here are a few things to think about to ensure employees feel respected:

- Do you always treat people with courtesy, politeness and kindness?
- Do you encourage every member of the team to express his or her opinions and ideas respectfully and courteously?
- Do you treat cases of genuine bullying and harassment with urgency and firmness?
- Do you ensure that neither you nor any other member of your team ever insults, name-calls, disparages or puts down colleagues or their ideas?
- Do you treat everyone equally and fairly, no matter their race, religion, gender, size, age, nationality or personality?
- Do you ensure that people are provided with equal opportunities to take part in committees, special projects, training and development opportunities?
- Do you ensure that you criticize in private and praise in public?
- Do you treat colleagues in other parts of the company, customers and suppliers with respect? How you deal with others will set a critical example for how you want the team to behave.

19

Warmth skill 4
Be more appreciative

Being praised makes us feel good and being praised often makes us feel even better. However, that praise must be earned, and it must be specific. Too few leaders praise enough, even though positive feedback is the breakfast of champions.

For more than 30 years now, I've been coaching the leaders I work with to praise their people more. It's been hard work, because so many of those leaders have found it hard to give praise, or to find things to give praise about. I can only deduce that it is because they all possessed the quality of being driven people, which meant that they thought nothing was ever good enough and everything could be improved. It was that drive that made them leaders but made it equally hard for them to find things to recognize and praise. They were too busy finding the things that could be improved.

Generally speaking, as leaders, we not only find it hard to give praise, we also find it hard to give feedback. I often hear how managers were sleepless the night before an appraisal session with a member of staff, especially if that member of staff hadn't been performing as expected. That kind of anxiety often leads to managers not giving any feedback at all. Neither positive nor critical. Why? Because we worry that if we praise people too much, we are going to raise their expectations of a big increase in their next pay packet. If we give them negative feedback, we risk embarrassing tears or angry responses, or worse, a visit from the HR department to tell us that we have been charged with bullying or harassment.

As Dale Carnegie, the famous self-help author, said: 'Criticism is futile because it puts a person on the defensive and usually makes him strive to justify himself. Criticism is dangerous, because it wounds a person's precious pride, hurts his sense of importance, and arouses resentment.' His suggestion instead was to always start with honest praise and appreciation. Let the other person save face and call attention to their mistakes indirectly, by asking questions instead of making statements. Always make a fault seem easy to correct and make sure your employee is happy about doing things you suggest. Carnegie said: 'Praise the slightest improvement and praise every improvement.' He suggested that we always give the other person a fine reputation to live up to.

It's hard to improve on that decades-old advice. We know from our own experience that we enjoy positive feedback and we really, really don't like critical feedback. Not unless it's delivered in a constructive and helpful way, with empathy and understanding.

Praise triggers neurochemicals that enable creativity

Being praised boosts our self-esteem and our engagement, because it triggers the release of dopamine, the neurotransmitter that helps control the reward and pleasure centre of the brain. Dopamine also contributes to innovative thinking and creative problem-solving. It is win–win. These effects, however, are short-lived, which is why the leaders who are considered most effective are the ones who are giving feedback regularly, heavily biased to recognizing good work and encouraging improvement.

When managers are effective at recognizing their employees, they are not only more trusted, but they have lower staff turnover rates than other managers and achieve better results. There is a caveat, however. The praise must be deserved, for empty praise has little or no value – in fact, it can reduce a leader's credibility. It can do more harm than no praise at all.

We want feedback that is positive and fits with our view of our performance. We don't want critical feedback that is unhelpful or useless. We need to know exactly what alternative behaviours look like, and why they will produce better results. We don't want praise for our personal characteristics, though that is nice; we would much rather have advice that was specifically about behaviours, either ones that are desirable or ones that will not be helpful in future. Instead of telling us what we are doing wrong, focus rather on what we should do instead, in detail, if you want an improvement.

'That was a good job on the sales assignment,' is too general, and yet this is exactly where leaders fall down because this is how they so often give praise. Positive feedback needs to be specific and needs to be timely. Instead of this generalized statement, be more specific. Your praise will be appreciated even more if you said: 'I love the work you did on why consumers don't go into stores any more. It was the key insight that gave us the edge in our sales pitch. Great job.'

Charismatic leaders spend time trying to catch people out on the good work they do, not on the bad work. Their praise is sincere and heartfelt, and it is frequent and varied. They will have thought about the role every member of the team played in a winning effort and will be sure to specifically recognize that role. Each and every time something good happens. Their praise takes many forms. It might be delivered in a one-to-one meeting in the corridor. It might be publicly recognized at a team session. It might be in a personal handwritten note.

Good leaders create a culture of recognition. They encourage employees to bring them examples of great work, so that they can praise people. Better yet, they encourage employees to recognize each other. They regularly remind people how they feel when they're at their best and encourage them to visualize those moments to enable them to repeat them.

Praise the unsung heroes

It is easy to recognize heroes, but affective leaders look for ways to praise the unsung heroes, the reliable backroom boys and girls who made everything possible but were not individually able to shine. One manager who worked for me always impressed me when he would go to our IT department after a new client pitch. He would tell them that we won that pitch in part because the IT department had done such a good job in ensuring that the presentations went smoothly and without a hitch. Next time he asked for a special effort from the IT department, he never had a problem getting the technical people to go above and beyond.

He also talked to the receptionists and told them how their warm greetings and helpfulness had wowed the client. That not only put a smile on their faces when receiving the praise, it ensured they would be smiling heartily at other clients when they came in our door. I would often hear him really digging into work to find out what people had done and why what they did was important. Then he would go out and praise someone.

He was also brilliant at coaching his teams to better performance. He would never offer criticism himself, but in any team review he would start by praising what had gone well. He would then ask members of the team to suggest ways that they could make it even better next time. He would often counter critical comments by suggesting they were being too harsh on themselves, but still nudging them to improve. I always thought that was a brilliant trick – he got them to be self-critical and then built them up, focusing them on the improved ways of doing things. Although now aware of an area for improvement, members of his team still felt the nourishing effect of his praise.

Charismatic leaders are strength finders. They look for the strengths in others and look for ways to enhance those strengths. They bring together the strengths of all of their team members and ensure that everyone on the team knows what each other's strengths are. When you link great work to a person's strength, you become more effective in giving praise. For example: 'Anna, I know how creative you've always been, and those illustrations for our sales pitch this morning really brought the data to life. Well done, we wouldn't have won that proposal without you.' You've done three great things in here – you've used her name, you've identified her strength, and you've related it to specific work in a timely way.

Great leaders always find a way to link good work to the purpose of the organization. We all want to feel that what we do is meaningful, and that what we do is important. It is soul destroying to believe that all the effort we put in is neither recognized nor worthwhile. When you are both specific in your praise, and you link it to a higher purpose, you are now operating at a very high level of praise giving. Something like this: 'You did a great job today finding a way to get that part to our maintenance people. That was so important. Had they not got that part we would have disappointed a customer, and we would have failed in our mission to be the best service organization in the world.'

Praise that is specific, timely, sincere, linked to a person's strengths and connected to the purpose of the organization is high praise indeed.

Don't fall into the trap of being quick to criticize and slow to praise. Most managers believe themselves to be more effective when they give criticism, and vastly underestimate the power of positive reinforcement. Ask an employee how they feel, however, and they'll tell you that too much negative feedback diminishes a leader in their eyes. Bosses who respect them, recognize them and encourage them are the ones they will always rate the highest.

Here's your appreciation checklist:

- Do you avoid giving feedback either positive or negative?
- Do you criticize more than you praise?
- Do you praise members of your team frequently enough?
- Do you give constructive feedback, always leaving employees feeling good about it?
- Do you constantly look for strengths and good work in order to give timely recognition?
- Do you make your praise specific?
- Do you link your praise to the purpose of your organization?
- Do you praise everyone evenly enough, even unsung heroes?
- Do you praise person-to-person, and publicly? Do you send letters of praise?
- Do you encourage a culture of praise and recognition?
- Do you give people 'a fine reputation to live up to'?

20

Warmth skill 5
Be more inclusive

Charismatic leaders know that relationships are the engines of success, so they are inclusive, in every way. They encourage diversity. They encourage involvement from all members of the team. They even encourage involvement from customers and suppliers, knowing that diversity of thinking leads to more creativity and to better results. They even include their teams in leadership itself.

Inherently, we know that inclusivity is a 'good thing'. However, I don't believe we always understand that inclusivity has many dimensions to it. At its most basic level, it is about including every individual who is a member of a team and giving them a sense of belonging and equality, no matter their age, ethnicity, nationality, religion or gender.

Inclusivity is about encouraging diversity, with all of the benefits that a wide range of experience, points of view and ways of thinking will bring to a team. Inclusivity is about a team of very different but equal people sharing ideas and throwing down challenges because they feel safe and included and encouraged to do so.

Inclusivity is also about bringing all of your stakeholders into your decision-making process, whether it be customers, suppliers, colleagues from other parts of the business, or anyone else who makes a contribution to your success.

In addition, inclusivity is about including people in leadership itself. Good leaders create a brilliant team of followers. Great leaders – charismatic leaders – create around them a team of leaders.

As leaders, we get things done through others, so the more we include them in our plans, our culture and our way of doing things, the more likely we are to succeed. If we are truly inclusive, our mindset will be to create a leader out of every member of our team. Great leaders create more leaders. The more leaders you have, the better your chances of success.

Every employee needs to have leadership mindset in order to be able to take the action necessary to quickly satisfy customers, deal with issues and make things happen, without having to go up and down a complicated chain of command.

They can only do this if they're included in thinking about strategy, goals, success measures and have in their minds a vision of long-term success. They can only do this if they feel included in achieving the purpose and vision of the organization. They can only do this if they understand not only the what, but the how and why. They need to understand the culture and values of the organization so that they can make appropriate decisions. They need to know why they're doing things, why it is important and what success looks like.

If all of those things are truly embedded, and each employee has a leadership mindset, they will be able to make decisions that are good for customers, good for the community, good for the company and ultimately good for shareholders. Leaders who keep information to themselves and don't include everyone in their thinking will soon find themselves with problems mounting up to impossible levels.

Employees with choice buy in to change

We all often fall into the trap of thinking that people hate change. They may hate the word change, but they love the idea of choice. When leaders include members of their team in creating choices for action, there is very little need to get them to buy into what needs to be done. It is their suggestion and all you have to do is get out of the way.

Charismatic leaders who do this shine because they're not being held back by pride or fear. They don't worry about whether the people they lead will develop and get into a position to take their job. They know that team members who can replace them enable the leaders themselves to progress higher up the chain. You can't be promoted if you can't be replaced.

To be truly inclusive, we have to change our mindset and ensure that we live the value of inclusivity in everything we do, every day. We have to watch for those inbuilt biases that may inhibit how we think about people. Each of us will have been brought up in ways that will have built unconscious bias into us, and to be truly inclusive, leaders have to search for and understand their own biases in order to prevent them from getting in the way of being truly inclusive.

You have to regard everyone as equal, and that everyone has strengths, no matter where they come from, how old they are, no matter their gender, race or nationality. Charismatic leaders always use inclusive words. It is always about *us*. *We* achieve this. They use gender-inclusive language, and they avoid generalizations or stereotypes. They don't make sweeping statements about social groups, nor do they make personal assumptions based on gender or culture, age or social group.

To be more charismatic, good leaders take time to educate themselves about the words and phrases and perspectives that might offend. They cultivate a mindset that everyone has strengths, and everyone is equal, which means everyone should be included. Everyone has something to bring to the party.

Innovation is better with diverse teams

Inclusive leaders make sure that, when meetings are held, everyone is equal and everyone is involved. They know that better discussions are driven by diversity. Better discussions lead to better insights, which lead to better decisions. Better decisions lead to better plans and better outcomes. Not one of us is smarter than all of us. They know that differences can be challenging but encourage members to be respectful of different views. They nurture respectful disagreement and debate. This is why inclusive leaders always ensure that everyone in the team feels included, and never allow bad behaviour, which marginalizes or isolates anyone in the team.

Inclusive leaders seek to create a sense of community and build relationships for the long term. They know that relationships are the engines of success.

Inclusivity and diversity enable teams to out-think and out-perform more homogeneous organizations, all the time. Workplace diversity delivers a far higher degree of innovation, has a hugely positive effect on company culture, and also has the less visible but no less important benefit of being able to diversify a customer or client base. All that leads to huge increases in revenue and productivity.

This is the inclusive leader's checklist:

- Do you genuinely believe inclusivity is a good thing? Do you behave in an inclusive way every day?

- Do you examine your unconscious biases, and seek to change them and the words you use in order to be more inclusive?

- Do you encourage diversity and take action to promote it?

- Do you strive to make every member of your team feel included and promote a culture of inclusivity in the team?

- Do you include your team in the leadership of your organization, and encourage them to develop their leadership mindset and skills?

- Do you include everyone in your vision and goal-setting, and then ensure they know what to do because they understand their role and what decision-making powers they have to deliver the vision?

- Do you include all of your key stakeholders from outside your team when you are problem-solving or trying to create new solutions and new ideas? Do you believe in the idea of co-creation as the route to the best possible solutions?

PART FIVE
Drive

21

How a cause can power
your charisma

*When leaders have a cause that inspires them, their restlessness
to achieve it becomes a tangible force, and their passion is like
a contagion that inspires, and liberates and aligns those around
them. Because of their drive, they radiate charisma.*

For Ken, working life had been pretty cushy for 15 years. As head of a service department within a nationwide engineering and manufacturing organization, his days were predictable and safe. He led a team of 45 people across six different locations, all providing office support services for the colleagues who worked on those sites. Approaching the age of 50, he was already starting to look forward to mandatory retirement at 55. They had their systems, they had their processes and they had a captive market, so all he really had to manage was workflow. Given that he managed a significant department that was a central overhead, he couldn't afford to pay huge salaries, which meant he didn't always have the best of talent, but his customers seldom complained, and he enjoyed life.

Then came the thunderbolt – the powers that be had decided to shut his unit so that in future they could buy their support services on the open market, at what they thought would be more competitive prices, for more creative work. They would consider selling him the business, with guaranteed contracts for work from them, as an alternative to shutting down the unit. Ken was shaken to his core, as was his entire team. All they had ever known was the safety of their jobs, and now everything was under threat.

Soon, however, Ken got over his shock and began to see possibilities. He realized that, with guaranteed contracts, he had a level of income that he and his team could build on, and they could begin to test their mettle against competitors, while already possessing a client base that was rock solid for at least three years. Far from the end of his world, this soon began to seem like the beginning of a new and more exciting world. He persuaded his four management colleagues that they could all buy into the business, as could other colleagues, and create their own countrywide agency – a start that other competitors could only dream of having.

A dream not a nightmare

Ken now had a dream to establish the most technologically advanced support services business in the country, serving local businesses as well as his former colleagues. They had offices, they had a captive market and they had all the technology they needed. He knew his customers were asking for more, and he felt he could easily give them more creativity, faster service and more cost-effective ways of doing things, using the technology at his disposal.

This wasn't a nightmare; it was a dream come true, a dream he didn't even know he had. His dream quickly turned to a burning passion and soon he couldn't wait to be freed of the shackles to start pursuing his vision. Slowly, by spending time with each and every one of his colleagues, by selling them his vision, by explaining to them that they could work on more exciting projects, develop their creative skills, and also benefit financially, he turned their scepticism first to neutrality, and then to hope, before finally lighting the touchpaper of their passions and aligning them to his cause. Even before the deal was done, they were selling their services to external customers and beginning to feel the excitement of new and different kinds of assignments. Their creative juices were being given a thorough stir.

By the time the deal was finally worked out, most of the members of his team were willing to put up some of their own capital to help fund the management buyout, such was their faith in Ken's vision. A handful of people decided it was best to take redundancy payouts and find another 'safe' job. For the majority that went with Ken, however, their excitement was a living thing, and it began to inspire even greater levels of creativity and effort, which began to reap them dividends in the form of even more work from their clients. Soon they were recruiting, and growing, to the delight of everyone concerned.

Ken, thanks his driving sense of purpose, had completely turned around the majority of his team, and built a thriving unit. He had gone from being an unnoticed middle manager to a compelling and charismatic leader, simply because he had picked up a cause to which he aligned every fibre of his being.

Leaders are compelling when they have a cause

What Ken showed was that leaders can only truly be wholly charismatic when they have a compelling cause. Without a cause, charisma could be seen as shallow, without meaning or purpose. When leaders have a cause that inspires them, their restlessness to achieve it becomes a tangible force, and their passion is like a contagion that inspires and aligns those around them. Because of it, they radiate charisma.

These leaders obsess about their customers, whoever those customers or 'end-users' of their services are. Leaders with a cause always make sure employees understand how their actions make a difference to the people they serve. This is true, whether those leaders are in business, in public-sector work or in charitable work. That, in turn, inspires them to even greater efforts.

A charismatic leader with a cause, and a conviction that we can achieve it, has a powerfully positive effect upon our brains. Why? Because, when we have a certainty about the future and conviction about our cause, we become more focused, more willing to collaborate, more able to learn. We become more innovative and creative, more willing to get involved and make a difference. Charismatic leaders give us a sense of certainty, because they paint a vivid picture of success for us. It is so powerful it almost feels like you are there already. This is how they use that future vision to drive actions today. They know precisely where they want to be in a given timescale, even if they do not know exactly how to get there. They work with us to determine the goals that we need to achieve if we are to succeed, and those goals become our goals, to which we are even more committed. Better yet, they ensure we all know exactly what our colleagues are doing and how we interact to achieve a great result, and that alignment enables better teamwork, greater agility and more innovation.

Because they know we are committed to the cause, charismatic leaders empower us to get on with our goals, and give us freedom to operate with autonomy within an agreed framework. As an employee it is reassuring to know that we have a way of doing things that empowers us and enables autonomy. Because we feel trusted, we are more likely to trust our colleagues, and that trust encourages open communication and much greater awareness of progress, problems or need for change.

Agents of change looking for trouble

Finally, because charismatic managers are never satisfied with the status quo, they are always open to looking to find ways to improve, so that they can achieve their cause more quickly and more efficiently. Any idea an employee has, any problem the team can crystallize, they welcome as a way to progress their cause. They are agents of change and they make every member of the team feel like an agent of change. Because of this, members of the team delight in finding problems that get in the way of progress, and the team delights in innovating to solve the problems. Now, they are in that perfect place, where they feel worthy, part of a team, delighting in their culture and striving to achieve stretching goals. They truly have a sense of purpose and that is not only good for their mental well-being, but also their health and resilience.

To align people to a cause, leaders need to learn how to:

1 Develop and articulate a compelling cause or purpose – see Chapter 22.

2 Bring customers into every team meeting and decision – see Chapter 23.

3 Align everyone's goals to a common vision – see Chapter 24.

4 Deliver autonomy through a freedom framework – see Chapter 25.

5 Drive for a culture of continuous improvement – see Chapter 26.

22

Drive skill 1
Develop and articulate
a compelling cause

Affective leaders know that a compelling cause does not have numbers in it. They do not start by trying to get the team focused on delivering a $5 million profit target, or a 60 per cent increase in revenues. They know that people want to do something meaningful with their lives, and that means doing something meaningful for others, so they start by defining what that is and why it's important.

All too often, people in leadership positions begin conversations with employees around the financial metrics and dashboard measures of the desired performance. They don't realize that this actually tends to make people close down emotionally, cognitively and perceptually.

Measures follow purpose and must not become the purpose. To open people's minds, you need to discuss first the purpose of the activities. When they emotionally connect with that, then you can discuss the measures of success.

Compelling leaders know that creating value for customers is the only way to create value for shareholders and all other stakeholders. Value for customers can take many forms – whether it is helping them make more of their lives, easing pain, providing joyful experiences, giving them ways to connect with other people, or impacting society in positive ways.

If you work internally in an organization, providing services to colleagues, it could be providing the means for fellow employees to more easily connect with customers, or giving them data that helps them to do their jobs better. The point is that, in some way, you are doing something that is meaningful because it is of value to other people – and the best leaders know to express their cause in this way.

They know that when customers value your services, you are able to deliver shareholder value, which is an outcome, as is profitable growth. Improvements in revenue, profit targets, market share – all of these are important goals, as well as being measures of success. But they are not the reason to come to work every day, and neuroscience shows that using any of these goals as your purpose does little to fire up the positive emotions of employees.

A purpose vs a vision statement

There is a huge difference between a purpose statement and a vision statement. Purpose defines why you exist – what you do that brings benefits to others and makes a difference to the world. A vision statement, however, can be about numbers – because it defines how successful you will be at delivering your purpose.

Let me give you an example, which I take from the Merlin Entertainments Group, Europe's leading, and the world's second largest, visitor attraction operator. Merlin Entertainments deliver some of the best-known names in global leisure – from Legoland Parks to SeaLife, from Madame Tussaud's to the London Eye.

They state their purpose as being 'to create magical, memorable and rewarding guest experiences'. No matter which part of the business, every employee can easily sign up to the idea of wanting to provide guests with magical experiences – a truly motivating cause to be passionate about.

The vision that Merlin Entertainments has, however, is different. They want to 'Beat the Mouse!' While not immediately obvious as a vision statement with numbers, the goal is to overtake Disney as the world's biggest visitor attraction operator. And that has all sorts of numbers attached – whether they be in the number of locations, number of visitors, revenues, profitability or even capital value. They will know absolutely whether they have achieved their vision or not. Equally, from daily customer feedback, they will know whether they are successfully delivering their purpose. Two different things, but hugely important when charismatic leaders try to inspire their followers. Each can be measured, but the measures are not the stated intent.

Purpose inspires customer-caring staff

The best purpose statements clearly articulate the benefit that you are delivering to your customers or end-users, whoever they may be. Merlin's purpose is to provide experiences of happiness or wonder. It could be to inspire exploration, it could be about giving people more confidence, security or vitality, or it could be changing the world by saving energy, reducing waste or providing education to the poor.

It pays to think clearly about articulating this purpose statement, and this is a key task of leadership. A purpose stays constant even while strategies may change and adapt to a changing world. There is considerable research to show that leaders who focus their purpose on making their customers' lives better are more likely to inspire truly customer-centric staff, who then work hard to keep those customers coming back, thus out-performing competitors.

The best purpose statements take customer focus to new levels, because they resonate with customers and emphasize the importance of serving those customers (and understanding their needs), but also because they put managers and employees into customers' shoes. They need to make employees want to get out of bed in the morning for a reason other than to earn a living.

Consider the following mission statements from these 21st-century companies as a way to help frame your own thinking:

- TED : To spread ideas.
- pawTree (a social-selling pet-care company): To create a world filled with unconditional love where pets and their people thrive.
- ABVI (Association for the Blind and Visually Impaired.): I Lost My Sight, Not My Vision.
- GoldieBlox (a toy company for girls): To correct the gender imbalance in engineering.
- Airbnb: To connect millions of people in real life all over the world, through a community marketplace – so that you can Belong Anywhere.
- Whole Foods: Helping to support the health, well-being and healing of both people and the planet.
- Tesla: To accelerate the World's Transition to Sustainable Energy.
- Uber: To ignite opportunities by setting the world in motion.

Please note that the shortest of these purpose statements is just 12 words. I've seen some incredibly powerful statements no longer than five words. A great purpose statement is compelling, tight and clearly delivers a customer benefit. What would your purpose statement be? Do you already have one in the company that employs you? If so, have you localized that for your own team? Have you given your own unit a sense of purpose that aligns with the purpose of the wider entity? Aligning them with the purpose of the corporation is critical, just as it is to align goals with long-term objectives. If you are in a big organization, why does your unit exist, and how does it help the wider entity to fulfil its purpose? Let me give you an example.

A broomstick to the moon

One of my favourite stories has to do with the NASA mission statement. In May 1961, the then president of the United States of America, John F Kennedy, said: 'I believe this nation should commit itself to achieving the goal, before this decade is out, of landing a man on the moon and returning him safely to earth.'

Later, on a visit to NASA headquarters, Kennedy stopped to talk to a man who was holding a mop. 'And what do you do?' he asked. The man, a janitor, replied: 'I'm helping to land a man on the moon, sir.' Intrigued, President Kennedy asked him how. The janitor replied that it was his job to ensure the morale of astronauts was kept high whenever they needed to refresh after their gruelling training programme. He provided the cleanest, brightest, most relaxing restrooms possible. By helping to keep their morale high this way, he was contributing to the mission to land a man on the moon.

I honestly don't know whether this story is true – but I've heard it repeated to me so many times by so many different people, that it has gained the stature of being 'a fundamental truth'. It serves to illustrate a vital issue for so many leaders, which is that it is critical to link individual purpose with that of the purpose of the organization to truly motivate every member of the team. In the case of the NASA janitor, he not only knew what the mission was, but he knew how to articulate what *his* purpose was in delivering the mission.

So, no matter where you reside in an organization, it is always worth articulating your team's purpose and checking in with the team to see whether this does motivate them. For example, one IT department I knew framed their purpose this way: 'Our company exists to provide first-class consulting services to our clients. *We* provide an always-on service to ensure our colleagues can do that job better, faster, more safely and in less time than their competitors.'

Leaders are made more charismatic when they frame their purpose in a way that has emotional appeal and is therefore more meaningful. They recognize that we want to do something meaningful for others, rather than focus only on profit and loss. Everything they do is then about trying to ensure everyone can deliver that purpose, to the standards that they set, and in order to achieve the vision. The passion they have to deliver their purpose powers them through challenges when things get tough. That determination is inspiring.

It enables them to be purposeful even when they don't have all the answers. It gives them a level of clarity and conviction, and that conviction provides the fuel even when problems arise. A charismatic leader has the confidence to say they don't have all the answers, and to seek those answers from the team, but their commitment to finding a solution always ensures progress.

Does your purpose inspire customers?

Truly charismatic leaders connect with their customers by checking that their purpose statement resonates with them and has meaning for them. I have interrogated companies who tested their purpose statements with groups of customers and then went on to change them as a result. By way of example, First Utility, when it started, was an independent supplier of gas and electricity in the UK. They first expressed their purpose as being to use technology to help customers understand their consumption better and thus be able **to use less energy**. Through focus groups, they quickly understood that consumers didn't like the idea of using less energy. This made them feel they had to make compromises and give up comforts. They far preferred the idea that technology could help them **to waste** less energy, which was a more accessible and positive way to express the company's purpose. By being sensitive to how customers received this message, First Utility was able to tailor their purpose statement in a way that resonated with customers and drove customer acquisition and loyalty. First Utility has now been acquired by Shell, and operates as Shell Energy.

People want to do something meaningful with their lives, and that means doing something meaningful for others. So affective leaders do not start by getting the team focused on numbers. They start by defining a compelling cause and why it's important.

To better tune your purpose statement, consider the following questions:

- Do you have a cause for yourself and your team that excites both your and their passion?

- Does your cause make a difference to other people? Have you expressed your cause (or purpose) in a way that makes clear the benefits that others will derive from your products or services?

- Have you connected your team's purpose to the purpose of your employer? Is there a clear link to show how what your team does, enables the achievement of your company's cause?

- Is your purpose statement short and compelling?

- Does your purpose statement help to guide your decisions and daily behaviours?

- Have you asked your team whether this is sufficiently motivating to help them out of bed in the morning? How do they feel about it? What would they prefer?

- Does your purpose statement have numbers in it? If so, consider whether this may better be a vision or goal statement.

- Have you checked how your customers feel about your purpose statement? Do they agree with the benefits that you say you deliver them? Do they have a better way of expressing the benefits you deliver?

23

Drive skill 2
Bring customers into every team meeting and decision

Charismatic leaders are obsessed with customers. They love to meet them, to understand their needs and lives, and bring those needs and experiences back into the team so that every decision can be more focused on how to improve that service to customers.

When you introduce employees to the people they serve, it unleashes high performance in ways that even the most charismatic of managers find difficult to unlock. Of course, people in the front line of retail stores, for example, touch customers on a daily basis. Restaurant waiters, hotel staff and railway staff on platforms – they all meet and greet and interact with customers every day. We sometimes forget, however, that not everyone experiences the customer. Or, even if they do, those customers who do talk to them are more likely to complain than talk with them about the benefits they derive from the service or product.

There's nothing better than having a real customer to give that more positive point of view. Those customers can tell all employees in the value chain how they feel about their products and services, and how they benefit from them. It is the connection to the emotional benefit that customers feel that drives high levels of engagement. By doing this, you connect the daily tasks carried out by employees to the deep-rooted need to be of service and to help others. They literally feel how customers feel and this has an emotional punch that enables agility and innovation like nothing else.

Charismatic leaders just love customers

For this reason, charismatic leaders just love customers. More than that, they are obsessed with them. They love to meet them, to understand their needs and lives, and bring those needs and experiences back into the team so that every decision can be more focused on how to improve that service to customers. Charismatic leaders know that experiencing how customers feel changes the way you feel, no matter where you sit in the value chain.

I always remember the impact of a story told me by Paul Polman, at the time the chief executive of Unilever, the global consumer products company. He said that the purpose of the company was to improve people's lives, which I told him I thought fanciful given that he was talking about soaps and detergents.

He told me about a visit to consumer's home outside Cairo in Egypt. He experienced her life and the hardship she had to endure as she cooked and cleaned for her family. She had to trudge for miles to fetch water, in order to heat it over a fire in a metal barrel and wash her family's clothes. She had to do the same again to rinse the clothes. She had to do it all over again that afternoon in order to cook dinner for her husband and family.

If Unilever could make a detergent that didn't need as much rinsing, or a cube of food flavouring that would more quickly and easily enrich her meals, they could make her life a little easier and give her more time – time she could invest in the children, start a business or spend with her husband. It might be a seemingly mundane product such as detergent, but it could still make a huge difference to people's lives, if you understood their needs. Knowing this, employees would be far more motivated to find solutions that would both be useful to consumers and valuable to the company.

Charismatic leaders find ways to connect everybody with the customer. Whether it's a parts manager in a warehouse, or a parcel deliverer in a van, they find a way to help everyone understand exactly what they are doing for the customer. To the parts manager they will talk about how failure to get a part in time to a garage in order to repair a car would impact on a mother waiting to collect her car and go to fetch her children from school. Without that part in the right place at the right time the mother would be disappointed and put in a difficult situation. As a result, she would likely never return. One moment of lack of care could have devastating consequences for both the customer and the company.

The purpose of your company or team has to be personal to individuals within it, and enable them to see how they are improving lives outside of the business you run. You cannot articulate a purpose that resonates with customers but fails to excite employees, and the way to excite employees is to visibly and persistently put the customer front and centre of everything that you do.

If you can't bring customers into your meeting, bring front-line staff in to talk about customer attitudes and highlight the problems or successes they see on a daily basis. Or, show members of your team videos of customers using your products and services, or better still, what their lives are like when they are unable to access your services. Survey customers regularly and bring that information to the table on a regular basis. Continuous feedback is key to continuous improvement. Tuning in to customers in real time is crucial in a world that moves at lightning speed. Social media means that any problems with service or product defects will quickly be brought to the attention of a wider world. Online, millions of people are talking to each other in a brutally frank way so we have access to a huge and hugely honest focus group that we can collect, collate and feed back to employees.

Tell customer stories all the time

Charismatic leaders tell customer stories all the time. They talk about great needs that must be answered. They talk about the challenges that customers face, and they make those stories a rallying cry for improvement and innovation. They also never forget the powerfully positive effect of happy customers, and they're always looking for great customer case studies to wax lyrical about.

They use these stories either to generate greater empathy and understanding among employees about what customers are facing, or they use it to motivate employees to work harder to find better solutions. Finally, they also use these stories to thank people and make them feel proud about what they have achieved, in order to keep them motivated to keep on going.

Charismatic leaders use their customers to help engineer a better future. Inspiring leaders are charismatic because they 'are' the customer, and they talk with authentic knowledge about the experience of being a customer.

Are you truly customer-centric? Check by answering the following questions:

- Do you truly put your customers at the centre of your decision-making and represent them at every team meeting?

- If you run a service function in an organization, do you recognize that your colleagues are your customers and ensure your team treats them that way?

- Do they understand their role in the value chain providing benefits to external customers?

- Do you bring customer feedback, insights or research into every meeting?

- Do you do this regularly to look for continuous insights that drive continuous improvement?

- Do you sometimes bring real customers into meetings so that team members can experience life from their point of view?

- Do you look for ways to convey the needs of your customers to your team, as well as the functional and emotional benefits customers get from your products and services?

- Do you *love* to find out about customer stories, good and bad, and relish telling them inside your team, all the time?

- Do you ensure that every person in your team understands how they are connected to the customer, and how their actions impact on customer service?

- Do you encourage your team to find and bring back customer stories that will help to problem-solve and innovate?

24

Drive skill 3
Align everyone's goals
to a common vision

There is so much power in clarity of vision. When people can see and feel and taste success, when everyone is clear about the future and have it in their minds constantly, they are able to save time and energy by staying focused and aligned. Charismatic leaders make sure the team's goals and values are in complete alignment.

You've started with your cause and excited people to it. You've put the customer at the centre of everything you do. Now, you need a vision of success that aligns everyone to a high-level goal, and you need individual goals that align every person to the high-level vision.

Without that alignment, your plans will never fully be achieved. Alignment helps the team to get things done faster, with less effort and with better results. Alignment helps people understand how what they do impacts on the result, and how what others do also contributes.

Charismatic leadership is about creating and enabling high-performing teams. That's why charismatic leaders spend a great deal of time talking about the future – in order to shape the future and to empower teams to achieve that future. Their vision is literally a picture of success, painted as vividly as they can, in a multidimensional way. It isn't just about the numbers, it's also about how it's going to feel and look, why it's important, and how everyone will benefit from success.

You have to explain to your team with crystal clarity where you're going, what they need to do and why it's a good thing for them and the people they serve. This means you have to be incredibly clear in your own mind as to what it is you want to achieve, over what period of time and what things need to be achieved in order to get there. You have to be explicit about what you expect from the people who are going to deliver those actions and you must take time to articulate a vision and share it widely.

There is so much power in clarity of vision. When people can see and feel and taste success, when they are clear about the future and have it in their minds constantly, they are able continuously to check and get feedback on progress and goals, and what changes need to be made to stay on track.

Charismatic leaders give autonomy to staff

Human beings work best when they believe in who they are, what they are doing and that they are part of a community of interest working together to the same goals. When a team is aligned around not only the vision and the goals, but also the values that will be used to drive behaviours, they become more empowered. Highly empowered, highly aligned teams will always do better. Autonomy is hugely important to people, and charismatic leaders find ways to give them that autonomy by creating a framework for freedom of action and decision-making.

That framework is comprised of a clear picture of success, stretching goals which are aligned from top to bottom, and a strong culture where values are used to make decisions, and are not just words on a poster on a wall. A sense of autonomy is liberating, and hugely motivating. No leader wants to have a team charging off in different directions, dissipating effort and causing friction and misalignment. They can only truly empower people when they are sure that every member of the team fully understands where they are going, how they're going to get there, what their role is in achieving the vision, and what values will be used to make decisions along the way.

Shared values enable trust and liberate employees to be leaders; they can then take action within a framework that enables speed, creativity and agility. You have to take care to define and live the values that you want, and make sure they are delivered in the daily behaviours of your team.

These intangible values, often dismissed as soft and fluffy, translate into actions on the ground, which then translate into hard numbers in the books. Leaders need to create more leaders if organizations are to thrive, and leaders are only created when they feel empowered to make decisions without always having to ask permission from their boss. Vision, goals and values enable that decision-making.

Organizations with rich, healthy cultures based on strong values achieve higher income growth than those with less well-defined cultures. As a result of strong cultures, those companies are also better at attracting the talent that enables them to keep generating growth in value. Leaders must choose their values with care and use them to drive conversations everywhere about not only their purpose and goals, but also the way in which they will be achieved.

Values are more powerful than rules

Values are more powerful than rules, because you can't provide for every scenario and when you get into difficult situations, a dense rulebook doesn't help to orientate people. Values and a sense of purpose get people on the right path. Values matter to employees and they look to managers to represent these values consistently. Culture is determined by the worst behaviours a leader is willing to tolerate.

You have a culture in your organization, whether you try to engineer it or not. It is in your team's behaviours everywhere – from the agendas for team meetings, to how you treat people, from how you treat customers, to what priorities you use to make decisions.

Alignment is a dynamic and ongoing process, so charismatic leaders spend a great deal of time talking with each and every member of the team to ensure that they understand the purpose, vision, goals and values. Alignment only comes from plentiful dialogue, and the sad truth is that many managers simply don't find the time or don't want to spend the time in the number of conversations that they need to create alignment.

Are you able to align your team members to a common vision? This checklist will help:

- Do you have a crystal-clear vision of success for your team? Over what timeframe?

- Does your vision go beyond the numbers? Does it show members of your team how life will feel, and how they will benefit? Does it show how customers will benefit and how many? Does it have emotional appeal as well as numerical targets?

- Do you have a set of high-level goals defined: 5–6 goals which are necessary to achieve the vision?

- Do you ensure that individual goals are clearly aligned to the high-level goals and vision?

- Have you defined a set of values to guide how you want people to behave in your team, particularly in service of customers?

- Are those values clearly aligned to your goals?

- Do members of your team feel liberated to make decisions in your absence, guided by your vision, goals and values? If not, what holds them back?

- Do you ensure that every person in your team has a clear understanding of the vision, goals and values, and has personalized them for their own unique role?

25

Drive skill 4
Deliver autonomy through
a freedom framework

When leaders create a framework for decision-making and empowerment, they enable their teams to be more autonomous. With that autonomy comes a leap in productivity. Charismatic leaders spend time inspiring the confidence in employees to make their own decisions and deliver exceptional results.

Nobody likes a micromanager. Instead, employees like to be given a certain degree of autonomy and responsibility for decision-making regarding their own goals and tasks. Employees who feel they are being micromanaged tend to have very low levels of commitment and engagement.

Those with high levels of empowerment have the highest levels of engagement – which shows that autonomy is not only good for the soul, it's also good for productivity, because it encourages employees to go the extra mile and feel accountable for their own decisions and actions.

However, when there are low levels of trust in the boss, employees tend to resist empowerment. Being trustworthy is the first step to being able to give people autonomy. Real progress only comes when every individual in your team is inspired to perform at his or her best and works as a member of a collaborative team to achieve your goals.

So, the trick is to ensure that they understand perfectly the purpose, vision, goals and values that you have defined as a 'freedom framework', within which they are fully entitled to make decisions when you are not in the room. The more empowered employees are, the more willing they are to give of their discretionary effort.

How boundaries give freedom

A freedom framework encourages decision-making and empowerment, because it sets boundaries within which employees can make decisions. Contrary to the concept of boundaries, these actually enable more empowerment because they make it clearer to employees what scope they have for decision-making.

If employees haven't been involved in devising their goals, your chances of motivating them are decreased. This is a worry, because you may have been instructed from above about goals that you have to achieve, so you have little room to enable your team to influence those goals. Employees expect their leaders to make decisions. What they want is more involvement in deciding exactly how they are going to implement those decisions. They want to have an influence on their daily activities. Employees will be happy to come up with goals that are sensible and even ambitious, provided they feel a connection to the purpose and vision. The more they been involved in those goals, the more committed they are to those goals.

A charismatic manager will spend a lot of time discussing the team's goals with the team. They will throw open the challenges and targets they have to achieve and be prepared to hold robust discussions on how best to achieve them. They will ask challenging questions that inspire creativity, rather than try to give all the answers themselves.

Once those high-level team goals are decided, the compelling leader will then sit down with each individual member of his or her team and discuss and agree their individual goals. Again, it is always best that the leader challenges and probes and encourages the employee to come up with the goals themselves, rather than lay them down step-by-step in a way that robs the employee of any initiative.

An empowering leader will hold goal reviews with the team often, as well as with individuals, checking in on their progress, challenging them, and constantly ensuring that they are on track with not only their short-term goals, but also the longer-term vision. They will be open to new ideas and encourage members of their team to be just as open, so that they can quickly deal with problems that arise and find new ways of getting to their destination.

The charismatic leader will constantly be reminding their team members of why they all originally set the goals, why it was important, and encourage them to believe in themselves when things seem too hard or even unattainable.

Spend time inspiring confidence in your team

Charismatic managers are not only confident themselves; they spend time inspiring confidence in members of their team, reminding them of their strengths and past successes and expressing their belief in that individual, and faith in their abilities, their knowledge and their worth. They make a big deal about giving them the authority to make decisions in relation to their own tasks. They find ways to encourage decision-making and will always question when a member of the team brings decisions back to their leader. 'Why did you feel you couldn't make that decision yourself?' they will ask, because they will be constantly looking for ways to remove any real or perceived barriers that prevent empowerment.

When managers reverse decisions that their employees make, those employees will feel undermined, under threat and undervalued. Worst of all, they will feel desperately uncertain. This will discourage them from ever making decisions themselves again.

Charismatic managers know that their employees may not always do things exactly the way they would like them, but they will bring their own flair and style to their activities. So long as things are done on time, to the right standards and with the right results, the way in which they're done is less important, unless it conflicts with the values of the team.

Of course, real empowerment is only possible when people feel fully capable of doing the job, and that they possess both the skills and knowledge to make the required decisions. Employees will think much more highly of their bosses when they are encouraged to develop their skills and given the means to find out everything they need to know in order to make decisions and act autonomously.

Praise more to be seen as charismatic

Recognition, rewards and encouragement are also hugely valuable in driving up levels of autonomy and empowerment. Managers do too little of this. Employees rate their managers as more charismatic when they are given frequent recognition. Being empowered requires individuals to take some risks, so being encouraged when they succeed will also encourage people to take more and more sensible risks in the future.

Hammering an employee when they take a risk which doesn't work will quickly lead to a lack of willingness to make decisions in the future. You have to forgive mistakes, providing those aren't so severe and so mission-sensitive that they defy any logic and sensibility. When the team can see that you forgive the right mistakes, it makes them far more willing to take what will seem to be risky decisions.

When employees feel empowered, they are willing to be proactive and lead initiatives to make things better for customers, more efficient for the company, or more beneficial for their colleagues. They become leaders – and it is a leader's job to create more leaders.

Are you doing the right things to create more empowered employees?

- Do you tend to micromanage? Be aware: this will not only lessen your charisma but it will destroy empowerment and discretionary effort.

- Do you overtly show members of your team that you trust them, and have faith in their strengths, experience and skills?

- Do you help every member of your team to understand the corporate story, the team story, and their own story, in order to ensure complete alignment with goals?

- Do you clearly give members of your team authority to make decisions within a tight framework, and ensure they are clear about the boundaries?

- Do you work with your team to set team goals, and ensure that they all understand how those are aligned with the corporate goals?

- Do you encourage employees to set their own goals, aligned to the team goals?

- Do you regularly review goals, and in doing so, are you open to new ideas and different ways of achieving those goals?

- Are you careful not to reverse decisions except under the most extreme circumstances? Do you let employees do things their own way provided the goals are achieved?

- Do you seek ways to develop the team and ensure they have the right skills, knowledge and experience to be autonomous?

- Do you frequently recognize and reward achievements, and encourage risk-taking?

26

Drive skill 5
Develop a culture of continuous improvement

Great leaders have a relentless drive to improve the way things are done, and thereby improve the effectiveness of their teams. When they involve everyone in a process of continuous improvement, that drive and energy is picked up by the team.

It was a great shock to Sally when she was appointed as head of the Talent and People Division of a major national consulting services business. The division was in decline while the rest of the company was growing fast, and she got the feeling that this was a last-ditch effort by the senior partners to find a cure for the problems that were ailing her part of the business.

With her usual gusto she piled into the challenge and interviewed dozens of her 200 staff to find out what they thought was causing the decline. She went to speak to many of their existing customers as well. She also went to speak to some competitors about how they ran their units and was surprised to find that not only were they happy to see her, they were also remarkably transparent in sharing the metrics they used.

What she found astonished her. She had expected to discover that customers were unhappy with the advice and service they were getting, and that she was going to have to recruit heavily and also reskill most the people she had working for her. Far from it, current customers were very happy, and expected to continue working with her consultants.

Most of her work was project work, which meant that she had fixed assignments that lasted for fixed periods and had natural endpoints. To keep growing, her unit had to keep winning new clients as well as win repeat business from existing clients. While they were fairly good at winning repeat business, the numbers showed they were appalling at winning new business.

Why? she asked. The clue came from one of her competitors, who had mentioned in passing that one of their key metrics was the number of meetings they held with existing and potential customers. The more meetings, the more business leads, and the more business leads, the more conversions into real opportunities and real revenue. It was purely a numbers game and her unit was simply not holding enough new-business-focused meetings.

Sally then suggested to her team that they had to establish a new metric for success that would be more important than all other metrics. It was going to be very simple – how many meetings were they holding each week that had to do with potential new business.

She instituted ways to collect this data and then made this number highly visible in all of her offices, updated on a daily basis. At first she was happy to put virtually any kind of meeting on the list, just to give visibility to the activity. Gradually she became fussier about what kind of meeting would actually qualify for the list – it had to be one that had to do with the potential for new business, and certainly not a routine meeting with a client.

Broadcast every good idea

Every day, she roamed between the desks of her consultants talking with them about what they were doing to generate new meetings. Every good idea Sally came across she broadcast to the rest of her team. As soon as something was proven to work, she institutionalized that as part of their working process. She held regular sessions with various teams to brainstorm ways to improve the way they excited potential clients to meet with them – and ultimately developed an intriguing narrative that helped to open more doors and interest even more potential clients in seeing them. The more they worked on this narrative, the more they improved it, the more success they had in booking new meetings.

Each and every consultant was given a target for the number of meetings they were expected to book each week, and they were given training on how to use the narrative effectively to intrigue clients and arrange a meeting. Gradually, the total number of meetings started to exceed all of their expectations, and the number of opportunities grew.

Their success rate at converting these opportunities into billable new business now came under scrutiny, as Sally realized they were woefully short of their competitors' conversion rates. Back to the drawing board for many brainstorming sessions on how to improve what they did. Now, Sally found her own staff were driving the continuous improvement process

Bit by bit, piece by piece, behaviour by behaviour, they improved their approach to pitching their ideas to clients and began to see their conversion rates improve. On top of a base of more meetings, an improved strike rate saw huge improvements in their income levels.

Sally now turned their attention to putting the same continuous improvement process into looking at how they could improve their business meetings with existing clients, in order to secure more work from them. After all, she said, it should be far easier and less costly to win new business from existing clients than to find completely new clients and win them over.

They discovered that they needed to broaden their offer in order to stay more relevant to clients after initial assignments had been completed. This led to new 'products' that would be of value to their clients.

Within 18 months, Sally's division was the best-performing part of the whole consulting business. Not only was her unit more financially successful, but engagement surveys found that her staff were more motivated than those in any of the other divisions and her customer satisfaction scores had improved dramatically.

Be visibly excited about good ideas

Sally's story is a great illustration of how charismatic leaders know how to get people to want to make changes and do things that are outside of their comfort zone. She knew that she would never succeed unless she got employees involved in the process, by exciting them to the cause and getting them to think about it every single day, in order to come up with improvements both big and small that would make a difference.

All she had to do was be excited about each and every idea that came her way and then give people a chance to experiment to find what worked and what did not. She gleefully held up each and every success, was fulsome in her praise of the team and passionate about the need to adopt a new successful process or behaviour. Continuous improvement became fun and was far from drudge work for her and her team. She hardly ever felt the need to have appraisal sessions with her team – they were so highly attuned to feedback on a daily basis that appraisal became a part of their daily lives. They enjoyed it rather than felt it to be an unwelcome chore.

When leaders have a relentless drive for improvement, an absolute certainty that everything can be done better, they enable the robust conversations that are the super-fuel of creativity.

Throughout the process, Sally knew that no matter what they did, the only result that mattered was an improvement in their revenues, so every initiative was always measured against this criterion. It was no good simply getting more meetings if those meetings did not result in more new business.

There are many methods of implementing continuous improvement processes – from Six Sigma to Kaizen. Nothing will really work unless there is a highly charismatic leader at the helm.

Are you delivering continuous improvement in your team?

- Do you have a continuous improvement mindset?
- Do you recognize that continuous improvement is key to a culture of change in your team, and the means to drive agility and innovation?
- Do you try to introduce a steady stream of small and low-cost changes in the way you do things, inspired by constant feedback from your customers and your team?
- Do you always try to get your employees involved in continuous improvement – do you make it part of their jobs?
- Do you recognize feedback is good, even when it's bad?
- Do you take pains to establish the right things to measure in order to achieve the right results (the numbers behind the numbers)?
- Do you use continuous improvement to stay relentlessly focused on improving the result – and do you ensure only improving the result is a good result?
- Do you see continued improvement as a passion or a chore?

PART SIX

Persuasiveness

27

How charismatic leaders connect and persuade

No matter how many people you lead, every day you will have to persuade them to believe in your cause and believe in the future you see. Persuasive communication is what turns strategy into action. Persuasive leaders are charismatic because of their ability to connect, communicate and inspire.

When Mervyn left the room, you could see 100 resentful pairs of eyes tracking him from the stage to the door, and you just knew that the rest of the day might as well be scrapped for all the good it would do. As CEO, Mervyn was arrogant, dismissive and patronizing. He had just lectured 100 of his managers about their lack of awareness of the financial realities they were facing, the needs of the company shareholders, and the need for radical change. They'd better be prepared to face up to the brutal truth, or ship out, he'd said. He had indulged in a good deal of finger pointing at the audience, using the word 'you' over and over again, frequently accompanied by the words 'not good enough'.

He was clearly worried about his next meeting with a group of key investors, and he had no time for questions. Mervyn quickly departed and left all of his key managers seething.

In the room was a mix of highly qualified engineers, marketers, sales leaders, customer relationship managers, operations experts and country heads. They knew only too well how difficult the market was. They felt they needed to spend more time helping their 10,000 employees to understand where they were going and why, and providing them with more reasons to believe in the strategy, before relentlessly trying to execute it. If they could spend more time convincing their teams, they would take less time delivering the change, they said. Mervyn had taken this the wrong way, feeling that they were trying to delay the inevitable and avoid the difficult decisions and actions that had to be taken.

Mike, the chief operations manager and effectively the deputy to the CEO, now stepped on stage. Mike had been in the company for more than 20 years and he understood his people. Taking centre stage, arms wide open and smiling broadly, he said: 'Right, that was fun!'

Charisma can change the mood in a room

To this day, I'm still not exactly sure why the audience burst out laughing. I was there as an external advisor, later to present a plan for a public relations campaign. I did not think that Mike's comment was a particularly funny statement, but his smile, his humble demeanour and his open recognition of the tense atmosphere was enough to change the mood.

Loyal to Mervyn, but acutely aware of the CEO's impact on people, Mike then asked for a show of hands. 'Who here thinks we have got the wrong plan?' he asked. He then invited managers to have a say, picking on people who he knew had their doubts. For the next hour he allowed people to vent, ignoring the appeals of the conference organizer to stay on track with the agenda. Whenever people were openly in confrontation with the plan, he would ask for their ideas on how they thought the company should better deal with the challenges that they had, and encouraged debate. Throughout, he showed his total understanding of the challenges they faced on the front line, never once dismissing people or dismissing their ideas. Slowly, it became obvious that everyone agreed with the plan. Their challenge was taking everybody else in the organization with them, which was essential if they were to succeed.

'We' instead of 'you'

Instead of using the word 'you', Mike used the words 'we' and 'us'. He talked frequently about customers and their changing needs, and told several stories about customers who had been frustrated by the way the company dealt with them. He used a mixture of logic and emotion, staying calm, cool and collected, no matter what people said.

When the central problem became crystal-clear – the managers needed help to take people with them – Mike called for ideas on how this might better be achieved. Several managers in the audience had had experience in a previous company of a change process which involved taking employees through a board game that helped them to better understand what was happening, why it was necessary, what they were trying to do, and how this would benefit everybody involved. Could they not get that consultancy involved in designing such a board game for their own staff? Mike agreed and promised to provide a solution within a week.

The rest of the conference ran smoothly and without a hitch, and by the end of the second day, Mike was able to tell all the managers that he had already located the change consultancy and would be seeing them the next day. A few weeks later, the change game was tested on the management cadre, who deemed it to be a game changer. They rolled it out rapidly in the business, country by country, with stunning success. Quickly, results started to improve, as employees got behind the plan and began to bring their own creativity and ideas to the table. Not only that, but employee ideas resulted in several other major changes in the organization, which brought major benefits to the company. Results were so positive that investor confidence returned, and the share price once again began to move upwards.

Great leadership requires the ability to persuade

I still believe that Mike's intervention at the leadership conference was a key moment for the company. His persuasiveness won the day and managed to get all the managers on board with the plan, in spite of the antagonistic start. I had never really seen his charisma before, but on that day, it was plain for all to see. Mike eventually did become the CEO, and Mervyn moved on to other turnaround challenges.

What I saw that day convinced me that great leadership requires the ability to persuade. You will have to persuade employees to work smarter and faster and more efficiently. You have to persuade financiers to give you more money. You have to persuade customers to buy more of your products and services. You have to persuade your bosses or colleagues to give more resources to allow you to carry out projects. You have to persuade colleagues to collaborate.

To be more persuasive, leaders need to do more of what Mike did that day and learn how to:

1 Understand their audiences better – see Chapter 28.

2 Facilitate conversations and encourage debate on difficult issues – see Chapter 29.

3 Take a stand with a powerful point of view – see Chapter 30.

4 Tell good stories – see Chapter 31.

5 Be a good speaker on stage – see Chapter 32.

28

Persuasiveness skill 1 Understand and connect with audiences better

Persuasive communication starts with an understanding of what it is you're trying to achieve, and who you most need to influence to achieve your objective. This requires you to know what you want those people to do, exactly, to help you get there. To be persuasive, you need to be clear about the benefits to them of doing what it is you would like them to do.

If you really want to communicate successfully, you first have to make a connection with the audience and understand what it is they need to hear, and where they're coming from. Then, you'll need to address those issues up front. You have to talk to your audience in the right tone of voice and in their language. Unless you do both of these things, your audience is unlikely to hear anything you have to say.

You may speak brilliantly, and deliver your messages with crystal clarity, but they won't have tried to understand you, and you won't have communicated. You won't have persuaded a single person to change their mind.

In business, communication is all about changing behaviours. Persuasive communication is what turns strategy into action. If you don't make an emotional connection, then you are unlikely to change the way people feel and think, and therefore you will be unable to change what they do. When people compliment you on giving a great speech, it usually isn't because of the brilliant oratory or the fine choice of words, it's more about the fact they felt inspired and moved by it. And that's about connection.

Successful communication is not about what you say; it is about what is heard. The acid test will always be whether people have truly understood you, what they take out of what you're saying, and whether you have engaged with them sufficiently to get them to turn ideas into action. This only happens when leaders spend time thinking hard about the audience.

What emotional state is your audience in?

Preparing for any communication session means first trying to understand where your audience is coming from. Do they feel antagonistic? Are they in a state of fear or uncertainty? You have to acknowledge the emotional state they are in, and the issues that concern them, if you want to connect. Just as Mike did in Chapter 27, rather than battle against negative feeling in the room, it's always worth acknowledging it. Poor communicators do little to adapt their message, tone, style and delivery to the needs of the audience.

What will interest them, what will make the connection, what will engage them and make a difference? What do they want to know? These are the questions to ask, before moving on to think about what people need to know, what you want them to feel and what you want them to do. Good leaders need to be able to think about and understand how people from around the world, with different belief systems and cultural roots, receive and process information: what filters they use to edit out as well as edit in information, what are their underlying, often invisible, assumptions that will shape how they hear and interpret what you say?

When people feel that you don't understand them or their point of view, they often think you might be talking down to them or at them, and your chances of bringing people with you will be severely diminished. Not everyone looks at the same set of facts with the same lens. People always listen from behind their own filters – filters which may be cultural or emotional, or they may be in place because of their unique perceptions and experiences, or even misunderstandings.

Persuasive communication is a process

Persuasive communication is a process. It starts with an understanding of what it is you're trying to achieve, and who you most need to influence in order to achieve your objective. This requires you to know what you want those people to do, exactly, to help you get there. To be persuasive, you need to be clear about the benefits to them of doing what it is you would like them to do. Until you have defined these benefits, whether they be positive rewards or the avoidance of danger, you have little chance of success.

You have to think hard about the people you depend on for success, and what motivates them, or frightens them or annoys them. It is only when you are clear and accurate about this that you can start to connect with them, by showing them that you truly understand where they are coming from. Why do they think, feel, believe and do what they do? How do you know this for sure? How are their feelings impacting on their behaviours? All of these are essential questions to understanding your audience.

Only when you have asked and answered these questions will you come close to being able to deliver messages that matter to your audience, in a way that is likely to persuade them to new and different behaviours. If your communication does not address all of these issues, then you will likely fail to make a connection, and you will fail to excite any change in attitudes and behaviour.

You always have to be consistent in your messages, but you absolutely have to tailor those messages appropriately for the audience. How is your core message relevant to the accountants in your company? How is it relevant for human resource specialists, salespeople or marketers? Same core message, but a different top and tail depending on the needs and issues of the audience. When you do connect, when you do have an emotional impact, your charisma quotient will rise, as will your influence.

Once you have crafted your messages, and delivered them, it's always crucial to check that people have heard you and understood. Too often, managers communicate with their people and then walk away, believing that the message has been delivered. Even if people have understood what you have to say, that doesn't mean they're in agreement with you and are now likely to change their behaviours.

Understand how they are reacting, or you have not communicated

To truly understand the impact of your communication on your audience, you have to understand how they are reacting and whether this is now advancing you towards your cause.

Some managers may be tempted to skip this section, staying resolutely focused on crafting their messages and delivering them with grim determination.

They would be ill-advised to do so. This is an area that employees rate their bosses most poorly at. Research by online polling company YouGov, which I outline more fully in Chapter 36, asked 4,000 people 'how well managers relate to their employees, in terms they understand'. The result was worryingly low – with as many as 55 per cent of employees saying their managers never do so. (More than 80 per cent of managers think they do.)

Successful communication is not about what you say; it is about what is heard. The acid test will always be whether people have truly understood you, what they take out of what you're saying, and whether you have engaged with them sufficiently to get them to turn ideas into action.

To be more audience-centric, always consider the following:

- Are you crystal-clear about what you are trying to achieve, and how *this* audience impacts on your ability to achieve your goals?

- Have you defined the problem in the right way, in a way that will resonate with this audience?

- Have you truly spent time thinking about your audience, about how they think, feel and act now?

- Have you thought hard about how people might be feeling, and how those feelings might be impacting on their behaviours? What is causing them to behave the way they do now, and what would better enable them to behave differently?

- Have you made sure that you will talk to them about their concerns, their issues, *before* you try to make them understand yours?

- Have you thought through the benefits of actions you propose, as benefits relevant to your audience? How, for example, will company growth be of specific benefit to them?

- Have you thought through who else might be talking to them, and what those influencers are saying? How would you counter those arguments?

- Have you checked what your audience has heard? Always best to do this during the conversation rather than later. This way you have a chance to correct any misunderstandings in the moment.

29

Persuasiveness skill 2
Have courageous conversations
that enable change

All conversations in leadership are, in one or other way, about advancing your change agenda. They are about trying to understand what stops people from helping you, what their needs and fears are, what assumptions they have that might be getting in the way, and what they know that is useful to share. They are about encouraging commitment.

So many leaders think that communication is about telling members of their team what it is they need to know and passing on information from above. It isn't. Great communication is about conversations. It's in those leadership conversations that the rubber truly hits the road. And it is only when those conversations are courageous and charismatic that employees are truly inspired. And yet, the majority of managers are uncomfortable with conversations, especially those that might have conflict and emotional outbursts.

In an online survey in the United States by Harris Poll, involving more than 2,000 adults, almost 70 per cent of managers said that they were often uncomfortable communicating with their employees, and almost 40 per cent said they were uncomfortable when having to give direct feedback about employee performance, particularly if they thought the employee might respond negatively to the feedback. A study by the Chartered Management Institute (CMI) in the UK showed that managers dreaded difficult conversations at work, more than having to have difficult conversations at home.

The chief reason for this fear was a lack of confidence about being able to persuade the employee, and that the conversation might become too emotional. Two-thirds of British managers admitted to becoming stressed and anxious in anticipation of a forthcoming difficult conversation. More than half would do almost anything to avoid having that conversation and would prefer putting up with a negative situation rather than tackling it. Surprised? Shouldn't be. The CMI study also showed that more than 80 per cent of British managers had never had any training on how to tackle conversations at work.

Person-to-person conversations

Charismatic managers are able to engage with employees in a way that resembles ordinary person-to-person conversation, and these daily talks with their staff enable greater levels of flexibility, more innovation, higher levels of employee engagement and very tight levels of strategic alignment. Their conversations are characterized by a more open and personal style, which these leaders try to make common practice throughout their organizations, knowing that they help to create collaborative and inclusive cultures.

Too often, managers think of communication not as a series of conversations, but as a process of broadcasting messages through newsletters, e-mails, corporate videos, internet sites and other means of 'push' communication. I know many managers who spend a great deal of time doing this, and then feel intense frustration that nobody seems to have heard them, understood or changed the way they behave.

Charismatic leaders know that to get people engaged and fully supportive of decisions, you have to go through a process of vigorous debate. This conversation may take longer than you would like, but in the end, you will implement faster and more successfully if you take the time. Leaders do have to set aggressive goals, but they won't achieve them if they don't sit down to discuss with people *how* to achieve them. Employees will want to talk with you about what their concerns are, and they want to feel that you are engaged with them. It's only when you consult with them on how to achieve goals that you create buy-in. And the only way they can have input into the process is if you sit down to talk with them about it.

If you want to be a successful leader, you need to take charge of the conversations in your organization. Whether you like it or not, conversations are taking place everywhere, and many of these conversations are either unproductive or potentially harmful. This is why a leader needs to shape and influence those conversations.

Conversations start before you enter the room

Charismatic conversations start before you even enter the room. They start when you think more precisely about what it is you're trying to achieve. You need to be clear about the intent of the conversation you want to set in motion. When thinking about your conversation, use these questions to guide your planning:

1 Is your forthcoming conversation about *informing* members of your team? Do they have and understand the information they need, to do their jobs correctly? In this kind of conversation, you need to plan how to give them news about changes, developments or new processes that will affect their jobs. You need to talk with them to see whether they understand fully what is now required.

2 Are you trying to *align* people to the strategy? Is this a conversation about ensuring that people understand better the team's purpose and values, what the key targets are for the year and what strategic priorities they are working towards? Can they directly translate these into their jobs? Can they translate the company values into their daily behaviours? It is these conversations that contribute to alignment because they help everyone to understand the purpose, values and goals of the organization, and more importantly, they understand how what they are doing delivers the purpose.

3 Is the conversation about *solving a problem*? Are you asking them for their views on what's going wrong and why? Are you asking for ideas on how to solve the problem? Have you identified the barriers that stop people doing what you need them to do?

4 Is this a conversation about *improving* the way we do things around here? How are we doing? Have we met our deadlines and quality targets? Are customers happy and if not why not? Are we getting the right feedback and information to help us improve our performance?

5 Is this a conversation about *implementing* strategy in the right way? Is everyone clear on what they have to do, and what performance criteria will be used? Do they understand when things need to be done by? Have they thought about who else they need to involve?

All conversations are, in one or other way, about advancing your change agenda, and reinforcing your vision and the vision of your company. It's about trying to understand what stops people from helping you, what their needs and fears are, what assumptions they have that might be getting in the way, and what they know that is useful to share. Mostly, great conversations are underpinned by far more important intent – which is to strengthen relationships, build the team culture and build trust and commitment.

In any conversation, a charismatic manager listens with intent. Absolutely the wrong thing for them to do is to go into meetings and express their view before anybody else has, as this will discourage genuine discussion and debate. The problem is, as people become more senior, it becomes more and more tempting to jump in and say what you think before others have. Charismatic leaders are not the ones in the meeting with the most to say. But they do know how to ask searching questions.

They always start from a place of curiosity and respect for others, and don't go into the conversation trying to be liked or respected themselves. The conversation is not about them, it's about others, so they have an open attitude and genuine vulnerability, which generates more of the same – mutual respect and shared vulnerability. They are supportive, and focused on the result, not the personalities.

Don't take it personally

Charismatic managers don't take things personally, because they know that if they read too much into the emotional outpouring, they will imagine slights and malice, which will merely make things toxic. Instead of taking things personally, they acknowledge that the others are feeling emotions, and recognize their job is to stay calm and measured and offer a release valve for stress, in order to progress to their goals. They especially know a conversation is not a debate, in which one side clearly wins the argument. They see it as a discussion, not a battleground.

When in conversation, whether with just one person or with many, charismatic managers know that employees want their ideas to be heard, that they want to be involved in making decisions that directly impact on their working lives. They work hard at getting everyone in a meeting to talk up and participate in a productive discussion. This means appreciating each and every person as an individual, and appreciating their views and ideas, by being genuinely inquisitive and interested. Charismatic leaders avoid pulling rank, as this will only encourage people to shut up. They work hard to ensure the people feel it is a safe environment to give them bad news and guarantee a no-blame culture when they do. Interrupting and being impatient are deadly sins in conversation, whereas recognition and encouragement fuel great involvement.

In any conversation, a charismatic leader knows it isn't only about getting people to talk to him or her. It is about getting them to talk to each other and encouraging productive conversations to take place everywhere. One of the great skills of charismatic leaders is to encourage employees to give voice to their imagination, especially during problem-solving or creative conversations. When a good idea is brought up, they latch onto it and move the conversation on to the best ways to implement the idea. They always try to create the clarity you need for action.

Any good conversation usually ends in a commitment to action. This means there has to be a discussion not only on the ways to implement ideas to best effect, but about who owns the actions, what performance measures are the right ones, what deadlines and quality standards are required.

Guide conversations, with care not to shut down people

Sometimes, leaders do have to guide conversations and put forward their point of view. There is always a danger of interrupting too much and shutting down the need employees have to express their views, but a good leader knows when enough is enough, and will begin to seed the conversation with the goals or points of view that can guide the discussion. However, when leaders ask the right questions, 9 times out of 10 the employee debate that follows will lead to the right answer, without the leader having to give it. You just have to have faith in the people, and know that if you ask enough of the right questions, they will always come to the right solution themselves. I can't stress this enough: when people have had a say in the things that matter directly to them, they are always more committed to those actions, because they feel less like things are 'being done to them', and more involved and engaged.

When a manager has remote workers, it is particularly important to keep them involved and engaged with other members of the team. When people work together, they have a chance to have lots of micro-conversations, and these enable the frank and uncomfortable conversations that sometimes have to happen in order to deal with problems and progress. But remote workers do not have these smaller interactions, so charismatic managers spend time encouraging all the members of their team to interact and reach out to each other and find ways to regularly stay in touch. During videoconferences, for example, good managers always pay particular attention to involving and acknowledging members of the team who are participating from remote locations.

Turn up more often

Managers can drive up engagement even without skills training in conversations, simply if they turn up to hold more face-to-face discussions. Showing up for the conversation is far more charismatic then staying in your office and sending e-mails. As many as 8 out of 10 managers surveyed for me by online polling company YouGov felt that they talk frequently enough with their employees about how things are going. However, only 40 per cent of employees agree. That is 6 out of every 10 employees feeling frustrated about the lack of time they have with their boss in conversation. In spite of how counter-intuitive it seems, the more time you spend in conversation, the faster you will help your teams to achieve your goals.

Great communication is about conversations. It is only when those conversations are courageous and charismatic that employees are truly inspired and committed to change.

Ask yourself these questions to help improve the quality of your conversations with employees:

- Do you ever find yourself avoiding conversations with your team? Be frank. If you do, ask yourself why. Uncover what holds you back from these essential conversations, in order to be able to properly prepare yourself to have more of them.

- When you meet with your staff, do you tend to talk more than you listen? Do you need to think harder about the essential and insightful questions that will encourage people to speak up and stay focused on the right things?

- Do you think carefully about the intent of any conversation, before holding it? Is it to inform, align, solve, improve or implement?

- When in conversation, do make sure to involve everyone and encourage them to express not only what they think, but also what they feel?

- Do you stay calm and measured during these conversations, making sure you don't take things personally and allow your own negative emotions to show?

- Do you encourage people to bring you bad news, and foster a no-blame culture?

- Do you judiciously guide conversations that threatened to go off the rails, and try to do this with focused questions that keep people focused on the goals?

- Do you ensure that you always involve remote workers in the conversations matter to them?

- Do you always close conversations with agreed actions, and a commitment to return for further conversations about progress?

- Have you thought about asking for training in how to become a better business conversationalist?

30

Persuasiveness skill 3
Take a stand with a powerful point of view

In the thick of change and uncertainty, charismatic leaders know they need to take a stand to persuade others to their point of view. This means they have a view on things that matter, and must articulate that view in a compelling way.

Charismatic leaders show courage. The courage to show who they really are, the courage to be positive in the face of adversity, the courage to step outside of themselves and be more focused on others, the courage to commit to a cause with heart and soul. They also have the courage to stand up for the things they believe in and persuade others to their point of view (POV).

There is an essential difference between an opinion and a point of view. To my mind, an opinion is changeable. It is based on what you know and understand about an issue now, and you know that more information or insight could easily change your opinion. A leadership POV, however, is unlikely to be changeable. It is based on the things you truly believe are important, on the things you are prepared to advocate and defend, and on your view of the world from the position you occupy. Essentially, it is an expression of what you stand for. Employees need these points of view because a powerful POV can help them understand how you see the world, what you believe in, and what benefits will derive from what you are proposing. They need to feel the force of your passion and belief.

A powerful point of view is liberating

When you have a point of view on issues, it is liberating, and means you won't find yourself having to say things in the heat of the moment that you might later regret. It is for this reason that many leaders fail to express a POV on issues – and think it is safer to stay silent rather than say something controversial. I beg to differ. Not having a POV is more toxic then having a controversial one.

Employees simply won't respect a manager who doesn't have a point of view, who doesn't take a stand. This can lead to a lack of clarity, and a lack of direction. It can paralyse decision-making and cause high levels of ambiguity. Charismatic leaders inspire confidence, so charismatic leaders are able powerfully to express their points of view in a way which inspires others.

One of my favourite quotes comes from Michael Eisner, a leader in the US entertainment industry and for 10 years the CEO of Walt Disney Co. He said: 'The best leaders always have a potent point of view. What amazes me is that it is always the person with a strong point of view who influences the group, who wins the day.'

If you think about what he is saying, the key point is that a leader will have thought about their point of view on key issues, well before having to deploy their viewpoint. Too few leaders think about developing a POV. Well-articulated views can win friends and influence people and give leaders a much stronger voice in shaping the future. Once you have developed these views, they are liberating – you can use them in all sorts of occasions and situations and even look for occasions to use them. When you have formulated powerful POVs on issues of importance, you can talk to these with more transparency, more conviction and more passion. Essentially, a point of view is an expression of what you stand for and should follow a definite construct.

A powerful POV is more than giving expression to an opinion. It has to be authentic and consistent, unlikely to be swayed by other people's views. Opinions, however, can and should be influenced by others. A point of view is a conviction, and conviction is charismatic. A powerful point of view generates trust – it shows people where you are coming from and allows them to align with you. Strong points of view should always show how your own values drive trustworthy behaviours. One trustworthy behaviour is to bring uncomfortable subjects into the open so that they can be understood and debated and resolved. And if you do this, you need to prepare points of view on issues important to you, way before you might need them.

How to frame a point of view

Framing a point of view, to meet all of the above criteria, needs four key ingredients:

1 The first is about stating strongly what you think and *believe* and why.

2 The second part is about explaining how you *behave* as a result of your beliefs, to give credibility and proof to your conviction.

3 The third part is about articulating the *benefits* you gain (and give) as a result of your behaviours.

4 And the fourth is how you think others should behave as a result – a call to *action*.

When expressed in this formula, a point of view is powerful stuff:

Belief – Behaviour – Benefit – Action (BBBA)

Earlier, in Chapter 3, I gave a personal point of view on the power of respect. I said I was a journalist in South Africa during the time of the apartheid regime and that I saw first-hand the dreadful impact of a fundamental lack of respect by one race for another. I went on to say that as a result:

> I have a profound belief in the importance of respect. I am hugely passionate about the power of respect, and how the world would be a better place if we could all learn to respect each other and each other's views. Every day I practise the art of automatically giving people respect without them having to earn it, and that often pays huge dividends. A hot button for me, one that drives a quick and angry response, is when I feel I am being disrespected, or when I see someone else being disrespected.

If I deconstruct the statement, you can see that I start with a belief. I explain where the belief came from and why I feel so strongly about it. I also speak to my daily behaviour, as a result of my belief. I then talk about the dividends I receive – the benefits. The only thing I haven't done here is a call to action – which might be something like this:

> We need to make sure that we are always paying each other respect in the team, and that is why I want us to develop a code of conduct which ensures that we are always being as civil as we can be. This will make this a nicer place to work and all of us are more effective team.

This would be how you could develop your own points of view on critical issues using the *Belief–Behaviour–Benefit–Action* formula. This method is powerful because it allows you to assert your POV by stating your personal conviction, and not telling other people directly that they are wrong because of their attitudes or beliefs. It is also assertive because it calls for new behaviours from those you are dealing with. And that's what assertiveness is about – being a go-getter who changes behaviours and gets people aligned to achieving great things.

A strong point of view on issues makes you more charismatic and more authentic, because it helps people to understand the values that are driving your own behaviours and desires. Try it; it'll be a hugely useful tool in your assertiveness armoury.

Let me give you another example to try to bring it to life. To do this I'll explain my point of view that led me to writing this book.

Belief

We need charismatic leaders now more than ever. Why? Because we live in an age of massive and accelerating change, powered by the convergence of rapidly developing technologies. These technologies – from robotics to artificial intelligence, from quantum computing to a hyper-connected world of billions of sensors generating ever-increasing amounts of data – create opportunities and threats on an unprecedented scale. In what feels like a tsunami of change, organizations will only achieve outstanding results if they inspire outstanding performance from each and every employee, individually and collectively. Those employees who feel threatened by change will never be able to rise to the challenges posed by the so-called Fourth Industrial Revolution. Even now, a huge number of employees do only what they have to do to fulfil the obligations of their employment contract. They are not truly engaged in their work. Those who are truly inspired go above and beyond their contract because they really care and want to achieve stretching goals. It is these inspired employees who give companies a considerable competitive edge. In the gap between doing only what we have to do and going the extra mile lies the difference between acceptable and exceptional performance. It is in that gap that charismatic leadership pays dividends. Sadly, too many managers believe charisma is beyond them. I disagree. Charisma is the consequence of behaviours that can easily be learned and mastered.

Behaviour

For the past three years I have been researching charisma and charismatic leaders, and thinking about the ingredients of charisma, particularly as they pertain to leadership in business. I have been talking to groups of people at conferences and events in many countries around the world, asking them what they believe charisma is and whether they think they have it. I have been formulating my own views on the essential skills of charisma and testing them with audiences and validating those essential skills against comprehensive research on inspirational management behaviours, by online polling company, YouGov. I have been coaching leaders on how to be more charismatic and watching the effect on the teams when they display it.

Benefit

Whenever I talk about the subject, eyes light up and curiosity sets in. Managers who never thought about the subject before become intrigued as to how they and their teams might benefit from knowing more about charisma. When they try the techniques I outline, they become more charismatic and therefore far more influential.

Action

Read this book: you will better understand what the skills of charisma are, and be able to start to put these skills into practice. You will be able to measure your charisma and understand your own unique shape of charisma. You will be able to get 360-degree appraisals of your charisma done and develop your own improvement programme. You will be better able to transform situations and lives, and you will achieve better results.

Crafting a powerful point of view is easier than you might think, and more importantly, is worthwhile. Speaking out on what you believe in shows your followers that you have a moral compass and are worthy of their trust. It gives them the confidence to follow you.

Ask yourself these questions to help you think about having the right points of view:

- Do you take a stand for the things you believe in, even when situations are tense and daunting?

- Have you thought about the critical issues where you need to formulate a constant POV?

- Have you formulated a point of view on your company's purpose? Have you formulated a POV on your team's purpose?

- What of the 4–5 key strategic objectives you must achieve over the following years or even this year? Why are they important? How can you express these with a powerful POV?

- What are the values of your organization or team? What are the standards that you ask people to live up to? Have you tried to express these in the formula I have outlined: belief – behaviour – benefit – action?

- What is your own purpose in life, and how would you express a powerful POV about this?

- What are your own deep-seated values and beliefs, the ones that drive the way you behave? How would you give a powerful expression to each one of these?

- What is the single most important trend impacting on your business? Are there other important trends? How would you express your POV on these?

- What do you believe is the single most important thing that you deliver to your customers, whether they be inside or outside your company? How would you express a POV about their needs?

31

Persuasiveness skill 4
Tell stories that change everything

Good stories can drive action, shape culture and encourage change. They have an emotional power that has the edge over logical arguments, or factual presentations. To tell a story well is to be charismatic, so persuasive leaders master the art of storytelling.

Working as a crime reporter on *The Star* newspaper in Johannesburg, I had drawn the night shift. No one liked the night shift. As an afternoon newspaper, the building was packed with journalists, advertising staff, printers and sub- editors from 7 am to 7 pm. On the night shift, you were all alone in the building. That was fine, so long as you were busy. On this night, however, it was as quiet as a graveyard – which was probably why my colleagues described it as the 'graveyard shift'.

I had been on duty for almost 10 hours, and I didn't have a single story. That just wouldn't do. For the umpteenth time, I made my crime calls, ambulance calls, fire station calls, but – in one of the crime capitals of the world – it was an unbelievably quiet night. A sergeant at one of the city's biggest police stations, under my relentless pressure, told me that they'd had to tend to a young missing girl for a few hours that afternoon before her parents came to fetch her. He patiently described to me what had happened in a bored monotone. In the land of shootings, stabbings, bomb blasts, riots, armed robberies and violent fights, a temporarily missing girl was hardly a worthy story.

A moment of inspiration

I waited another hour before beginning yet another round of crime calls. My contacts snarled at me, now weary of my enquiries. With just an hour to go, I realized that for the first time in my career, I was going to end a shift without having written a single word. I thought more deeply about the missing girl and scoured my notes for a sliver of inspiration. All I had was a description of how the policeman in the station had worked together to keep the missing child entertained while trying to find her parents. Finally, I had a moment of inspiration. I wrote:

> Policemen are hardened to murder, rape and robbery, but not to lost little girls with big, weepy brown eyes.
>
> Just such a girl had the policemen of Johannesburg's Hillbrow charge office eating out of the palm of her hand yesterday. And the men in blue were in there vying for her attention with sweets and favours. Four-year-old Emily reigned supreme in the police station for nearly three hours while efforts were made to trace her parents.

I then went on briefly to describe how the policemen finally had to hand her over to secretaries in the office, in order to get back to their beats. A radio bulletin got her parents' attention and brought them to Hillbrow to take her home. My story was just 275 words long.

I posted my story into the news editor's inbox and left for home to sleep off my frustration. I had little hope of being in print in my newspaper the next day, but at least I had submitted a story! To my astonishment, the next day, on the way back into the office for yet another night shift, I saw placards on the street corners with the words: 'Big brown eyes had them off beat.' This meant that not only had my story got into print, but that it was on the front page. That night, I received calls from many of my contacts in the police and emergency services, to tell me how much they appreciated the story. It was the best PR they'd had in years.

Great stories are under our noses

I sometimes tell this story to the leaders I work with, especially when they tell me they don't have any stories to use in their own business. I use it to make the point that sometimes, great stories are right under our noses, if only we can spot what makes them different, what makes them appealing, what makes them worthwhile.

Stories can be the most persuasive tool in the communication armoury but need to be carefully chosen to achieve objectives. This means knowing exactly what you're trying to achieve with the stories you tell. Good stories deliver great truths, and appeal to our hearts, where logic appeals to our minds. What makes a good story?

Your values present a myriad of opportunities to story-tell. If one of your values, for example, is to be bold, you can tell stories about employees who took bold steps to change the way they did things, or to change the outcome for a customer, in order to reinforce the behaviours that you would like. Equally, you could talk about how a team refused to be bold, stuck with the status quo, and gradually became irrelevant, losing their jobs.

Customers always present opportunities for stories. In order to drive innovation, you could tell a story about a customer facing a challenge that has frustrated them, which they can't solve, and which is likely to cause them severe competitive disadvantage. That customer has come to you, because they are inspired by the creativity of your team. How are you and your team now going to respond to their need?

Describing how your team solved a customer's problem is another story opportunity. Tell people about how praiseful the customer is now, and how the customer is benefiting from the solution your team provided, to praise your team and encourage even more innovation.

Telling a story about how one of your values led you to a seminal moment in your career, or how one of your biggest mistakes led to the most important learning of your life, helps you to reveal more about who you are to your employees, helping you to build trust, or show vulnerability and humanity.

What's the format for a good story?

Stories are everywhere. They are in the needs of your customers, or the communities you operate in. They are in your strategy, your purpose and goals. There are stories in your values and behaviours – good behaviours and bad behaviours. There are stories in your products and services. Once you've found them, learning to tell them in a powerful way is the next step. There are many ways to tell a story.

What's the simplest yet most powerful format for a good story? I recommend you use the age-old *Problem–Solution–Benefit–Reflection* formula.

Firstly, describe the *problem* or challenge that someone faced. Make it as vivid as you can. Describe the unsuccessful attempts to solve the problem. When you think about the problem part of your story, you also have to decide on a character for your story. How does this problem impact on them? What difficult choices are they facing? When you lead with the problem, with the dilemma your character is facing, you automatically intrigue people to want to know what happens next.

Then, describe the Eureka moment that led to a solution. What is the solution, and how is it unique and special? The Eureka moment is always better if you can describe how efforts to solve the problem at first simply made it worse.

Thirdly, talk about the benefits that are now being derived from the solution. The benefits part of your story is all about transformation. How did your character change the world for better or for worse? This is the climax of your story.

Finally, you can always end your story with some personal reflection – what you took out of the events you describe. It is in here that the lesson resides. Look again at my story about my night shift on *The Star* newspaper – it is a classic construct:

Problem – I had no story, and the only story I had seemed trivial. Everything I tried to do to find one resulted in frustrating failure and made my situation worse! (I was really annoying all my contacts.)

Solution – I thought about the one story I had, differently, and saw there was a good story there.

Benefit – I got a front-page story and plaudits from my contacts!

Reflection – I learned a life lesson that still serves me well. Stories are everywhere if you look for the right angle.

Let people come to your message

This formula works for almost any kind of story. It enables you to package your message so that it can be understood – uniquely – by every listener. Try not to make the lesson too obvious; it's always best if people come to the message through their own deduction. That's why testing a story on a few people whom you trust, to see what they take out of it, is essential to good storytelling. You need the message in there, but not so obvious that you find yourself patronizingly stating the key message in the story. It's always better when people come to the truth themselves.

Most of us are already pretty good at telling stories, having been excited by them since childhood. As we grow older, however, we come to think that logic and PowerPoint is the way to persuade. We abandon stories, and then we wonder why we can't move people to change. Charismatic leaders tell stories all the time.

Charismatic leaders always, always, always practise their stories. The more easily stories flow, the tighter and punchier they are, the more impact they will have. By all means, season your stories with the spice of characterization, or of description, but not at the cost of brevity. Stories, I believe, are the superglue of messages and storytelling organizations are healthy organizations.

Good stories have legs and travel far. Unlike a PowerPoint presentation, people remember stories and will retell them, often. Through stories, people identify with tragedy or triumph, with hopes and fears, with values they value or behaviours they loathe. In this way, storytelling leaders become truth-tellers to their people, and bring meaning to their followers.

To be more focused on storytelling in your leadership, consider the following:

- Stories are the superglue of messages. Do you use stories enough in your communications?

- Do you select your stories with strategic intent? In other words, do you select stories that help you to achieve your objectives?

- Do you have enough stories to use? Do you look for stories that will help you get your message over in the right places?

- Do you look for customer stories to tell – stories that illustrate customer needs or good and bad experiences with your services and products?

- Do you look for stories from all of your stakeholders – from suppliers to local communities – that help you to deliver your messages?

- Do you look for stories in your vision of the future – to try to turn that vision into a story that people can relate to?

- Do you use your values, or the values of your company, to tell good stories? Have you seen things happening in your company that illustrate your values at work, or behaviours from people that are the polar opposite of the values you'd like them to be exhibiting?

- Do you use the *Problem–Solution–Benefit–Reflection* formula when constructing your stories?

- Do you practise your stories, and seek feedback on what messages are being taken from them?

32

Persuasiveness skill 5
Be a good speaker on stage

When you master public speaking, it boosts your confidence and makes you more charismatic. Speaking well on the stage superpowers your ability to influence, to win over the group, to motivate people to change, to win support for your ideas. In a modern workplace, it is perhaps one of the most important skills of all.

Public speaking is an essential skill for your career. The better you are at public speaking, the more you will find that this is a soft skill that delivers cold hard cash. An investment in your speaking skills will pay dividends for decades to come. Persuasiveness is today the number one skill of management, and being a good public speaker is a critical part of being a successful persuader.

There is a huge value in being able to change minds. Persuading customers to buy more of your products or services, convincing investors to put more of their money into your business, winning over new partners to help you in your ventures – these all result in more money in your pocket. Perhaps the most important audience of all, however, is your own team – the people you rely on for success. These people expect you to be good at public speaking. A clear message from the YouGov research, which I outline more fully in Chapter 36, is that employees won't find their bosses inspiring if those bosses are not inspiring speakers. Being proficient at public speaking is not good enough – you have to be impressive to make an impact.

I have coached countless senior executives on speeches they have had to give, presentations they have had to make to shareholders, to customers or to employees. I have myself given hundreds of speeches around the world. Here's what I've learned.

How to prepare for a talk

1   Always take the time to prepare properly for public platforms. You will never do a good job if you try to wing it, or if you don't put in sufficient time to do a great job.

2   Before you even start crafting your messages, spend some time thinking about the audience. What's most important to them? How can you show them how what you have to say relates to the things that they care about? How do you want them to feel? What facts do you need them to know? And what do you want them to do? What is your call to action?

3   Distil what you have to say to them into one big idea – and make that the theme of your talk. Weave that theme through everything you say. Try to distil your theme into one word. Is this a story about growth? About empathy? About agility? What's the key idea you need to get through to them? Imagine someone from your audience walking out the room and talking to a colleague. What words would you like them to use when describing what you had to say?

4   Write out your narrative before trying to turn it into a speech or talk. First, get everything you want to say out, then spend more time trying to get it right, by ruthlessly editing, refining and crafting.

5   Make sure you start your presentation well – you only have a few minutes to intrigue your audience and make them want to listen to you. Start with a good story, a truly intriguing fact or a thought-provoking question.

6   Lace your speech with a series of stories, each of which makes a point you want them to receive. This means having to think about the key messages you want to deliver, and the order in which you need to build a narrative in a logical and cohesive way. Once you have those messages clear in your mind, now think about the story that will do the best job of delivering the message. Stories are like stealth fighters, delivering your messages under the radar and directly to the hearts of your listeners. If you use only facts and figures, charts and diagrams, you invite them to

awaken their critical thinking skills, and in their heads, they will be arguing with you. Of course, there are times you will have to stick to the facts, and only the facts, but it is always worth trying to see if you can sneak a good story in.

7   Limit the number of slides you use, especially the wordy ones. The worst mistake you can make is to use your slide as your speaking script. People can read what's on the screen and will soon lose interest in what you have to say if you give them too many words up there on the screen to compete with the ones you're trying to deliver yourself. Use dramatic images, or illustrations that make a point, but don't ever give them a series of bullets, or they'll want to use a bullet on you.

8   Try to encourage audience participation. I don't mean that cringe-inducing kind of participation that entertainers force on you, I mean get them thinking by asking them rhetorical questions, or giving them a quiz, or asking them to take a survey and compare their results with the results of research you've done. Anything to get them thinking and engaged with what you're saying, rather than simply having to be passive recipients of your words

9   Always have a call to action, and make sure that you are clearly spelling out the benefits of what you have to say. Make sure that everyone will understand why what you have to say is important to *them*.

10 Make sure you have a big finish. Use a powerful story, or a killer fact. When people walk out the room, if you finish on a high, with something that cleverly summarizes what you've had to tell them, and you deliver that with passion and verve, they'll remember you and they'll remember what you had to say.

11 Always try to deliver your talk without reading it. Learn your narrative, then reduce it to a series of short and cryptic bullet points, which you can keep on a note that you hold in your hand, or place on the table in front of you, but which you only occasionally refer to in order to make sure that you are on track.

12 Rehearse and rehearse and rehearse. You can never spend too much time practising your speech, to make sure you deliver it well, that you stay on time (the cardinal sin of speech-giving is to allow yourself to run over time), and that you pay attention to your body language and stage presence. This means making sure that you stand or walk with confidence, that you occupy this stage in a way that commands attention, while

always making sure that you make eye contact with different members of the audience so that they feel you're talking directly to them. Let your nerves work for you, and use them to channel your energy and focus. Even though I have given hundreds of talks, I still feel nervous before every single one, and I try to encourage the nerves. That may sound weird, but I know that if I'm nervous I'm still likely to stay sharp and not take my audience for granted.

13 Don't aim to be slick. I would much rather listen to somebody who stumbles over words, someone who occasionally meanders, but who is passionate, humorous, authentic and interesting, than someone who is so slick that it almost appears inauthentic.

14 Smile, a lot. Speakers who are smiling – genuinely smiling – look pleased to be there, and you warm to them. The majority of speakers I coach are so busy concentrating on what they have to say that they forget to smile. It really does make a huge difference. (Of course, sometimes smiling is inappropriate, but I'm sure you will know when such a moment arrives.)

15 Breathing properly is essential. The one mistake I see, over and over again, is speaking too quickly and not taking enough time to breathe deeply and properly. As a result, your voice become tremulous, even squeaky, and you will sound awful. Pausing is good for a speech, and in those pauses, which may seem interminable to you, you give your audience a chance to catch up and reflect. In those pauses, you can breathe, calm yourself and re-energize yourself. Good speakers practise their pauses, and their breathing.

When you master public speaking, it boosts your confidence and makes you more charismatic. Speaking well on the stage superpowers your ability to influence, to win over the group, to motivate people to change, to win support for your ideas. It will help you to make a difference in your life, your business, your community, your career. Many people would rather die than speak in public. Charismatic leaders welcome the opportunity, because they know it will help them to differentiate themselves from the pack.

PART SEVEN

Understanding and measuring charisma

33

The chemistry of charisma

Neurotransmitters are chemicals found in the brain that communicate to the body and have a powerful effect on mood, on motivation and on our feelings of stress and anxiety. These neurochemicals, therefore, have a powerful influence on our behaviours. Charismatic leaders help to induce the right neurochemicals that encourage positive workplace behaviours.

Jonathon, a retired friend of mine, had a heart attack while out on the golf course last year. Two of his playing partners helped him back to the club-house while a third ran ahead to fetch help. An air ambulance helicopter picked him up from one of the fairways and flew him to hospital, where he was given emergency treatment. It was all very dramatic and unsettling, for everyone concerned. A little later, he had three stents put into his arteries to aid blood flow. He was given severe warnings about his eating habits and the need to lose weight. And, for a while, he did. Now the weight is creeping back on.

In spite of the sure knowledge that this is dangerous, he has returned to his old eating and drinking habits. He's not alone. I've heard the same about many heart attack and stroke victims. In fact, the vast majority of those diagnosed with a new chronic condition have significant problems adopting healthy behaviours – even after learning about evidence that such changes will help them survive. Denial can be psychologically protective, reducing anxiety as people distort warning signs to reassure themselves, that they are now not in danger.

If it is so difficult to change behaviours, even when it is absolutely certain that not doing so is perilous, how easy is it to get people in an organization to change their behaviours in order to drive a better performance? You can't threaten them with death, though you might want to. In any case, the threat may invoke the wrong behaviours, not the ones you want.

The answer lies in how you make them *feel... and this is the key to charisma and to great performance.* If you can make members of your team feel positive about themselves, so that they feel worthy, important and a key member of the team, your chances of change are a great deal higher.

We all want to be recognized

Yet, all too often, employees suffer from the lack of what they want the most – to be recognized for their individual contributions and to be made to feel important. Research done for me by online polling company YouGov among 4,000 employees shows that this need is far greater than any other. It is more important to discretionary effort than pay, than a good working environment, or even the vision and purpose of the organization. Members of your team won't find meaning in that purpose if they don't feel that what they do every day matters to you and the organization.

If you can help them to feel important and valued, if you can help them to feel part of a team, and if you can give them stretching but meaningful goals and a strong sense of purpose, then performance will skyrocket. Why? Because you will be helping to change their brain chemistry, and *that* will help them to behave differently.

This is the insight that comes from neuroscientists – the people who study the nervous system and the brain, especially in relation to behaviour and learning. The research they are doing around the world is beginning to piece together connections between the brain and behaviour, especially at work. What they have discovered provides valuable insights for leaders. Essentially, it comes down to this: the more leaders understand about how our brains function, and the chemicals they release, the more likely they are to successfully deliver their plans. As we will see, being charismatic is key.

The way we behave at work doesn't conform to the way many highly logical leaders expect us to, for we are unconsciously governed in ways that pure logic will never overcome. This is why so many change initiatives fail. We often hear leaders talking about the need to reach hearts and minds to enable change. They mean that we need to be both logical and emotional in the way we communicate and deal with members of our teams. What they don't realize, is that it is all about the brain. If leaders want successful change, they have to appeal both to our intellect and to the prehistoric neurochemicals in our brains, because these have a far greater effect on how we think, feel and behave than we have ever imagined.

The 80 billion neurons in our brains

Our brains are made up of a complex network of billions of neurons, which serve as the building blocks of the nervous system, transmitting information to and from the brain and throughout the body. Scientists suggest we could have up to 80 billion neurons in the brain. Chemicals called neurotransmitters enable information to pass between these neurons. Electrical signals cannot close the gap between neurons so instead they use chemical signals. Once those chemical signals reach the next nerve cell, they bind to its receptors and induce electrical signals, which travel the body. These neurotransmitters are the pivotal messengers in your brain, and they function throughout the body's central nervous system. They regulate physical and emotional processes such as mental performance, emotional state, physical energy and pain response. They are present wherever there are nerves, such as your gut and muscles.

No doubt you have heard about these chemicals – endorphins, serotonin, oxytocin, dopamine and cortisol, among many others. For example, endorphins mask pain and help you to recover when you have exercised. They give you a high, which encourages you to exercise again. Dopamine is the pleasure or motivation chemical. Everything that makes you feel good is down to this key neurotransmitter and the effect it has on the brain – whether it's eating, sex or happiness. (Addictive substances affect dopamine release in the brain's reward pathway.) Dopamine plays a role in positive reinforcement and making a person more likely to repeat actions.

It is worth understanding a little more about these chemicals and how they affect us. It is even more worthwhile to understand how our behaviours as leaders can induce these chemicals – both good and bad. That is the purpose of this chapter – to help us be more aware of what's really going on inside the heads of our followers, and how our charisma (or lack of it) can encourage either the right neurochemicals and behaviours, or the wrong ones.

One neuroscientist I interviewed, trying to keep things simple so I could understand, said that our brains operate on two axes. The first axis is about

FIGURE 33.1 The worthiness matrix

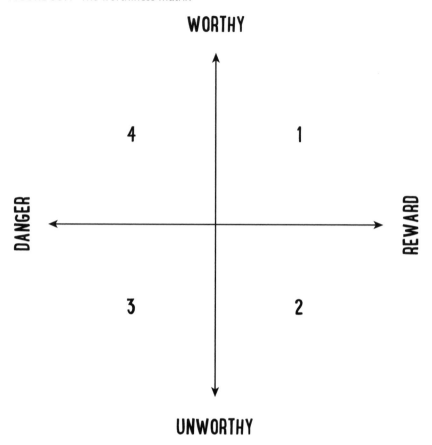

whether we are moving away from danger or toward reward. The second axis is about feeling worthy or unworthy (see Figure 33.1).

In all of these different quadrants, different neurochemicals will be at work, influencing our moods and our behaviours.

The worst quadrant to be in is where you feel both in danger and unworthy (quadrant 3). For example, prisoners in a jail would sit at the extreme end of this quadrant. However, employees who feel their jobs are in peril, or that they face massive change and upheaval, will also sit in this quadrant. When their boss fails to recognize them, or implies that their department is under threat, they will feel both in danger and unworthy. It is the worst place to be, and will result in poor performance, bad behaviours and a lack of results.

Employees who do feel worthy, recognized and valued, but who are under threat, will be able to perform well, for a period. This is the case, also, for employees or teams facing a crisis (quadrant 4). Both of these situations would be typical of those that people in the top left quadrant would be in. They feel good about themselves, confident in their skills, but sustained periods of stress will rob them of energy and fill their bodies with unhelpful neurochemicals. Good performance under stress is only sustainable for a short while.

When employees are incentivized with a big bonus, but are treated badly by their boss, they will become cynical, resistant and are likely to work to rule, even if there is a big pot awaiting them. They will store up their resentment and likely leave as soon as they have pocketed the bonus. These people are in quadrant 2.

Employees who are made to feel valued and worthy, and who are also working to stretching goals, and rewards which they value, will be in the top right-hand quadrant, and will be high performers, capable of sustained high performance. Charismatic leaders will always try to ensure their team members fit in the top right-hand quadrant. They will work hard to make employees feel truly included.

The biggest chemical hit is from danger

Our primitive lizard brains were wired to pay a lot of attention to anything that was threatening, an essential reaction to survival. We were also wired to seek rewards such as food and shelter, community and fun. However, we have a far stronger reaction to danger, because of the threat to life. We can always wait for food and water, but we can't wait if we are in imminent mortal danger.

We derive pleasure and meaning from being part of a community. Rejection and isolation are really bad for us. We are wired to check that there is someone looking out for us, and this need to connect stays with us throughout our lives, including at work. Our brains are constantly checking whether we are accepted or rejected, whether we are part of a group or out of the group.

The ideal state to be in is in the top right-hand quadrant of the diagram, where we feel both worthy and part of the community, *and* we are moving towards a reward of some kind (Figure 33.2). The worst place to be is when we feel unworthy, rejected and in danger, the bottom left side of the diagram. Unwittingly, managers can often place employees in the bottom left-hand quadrant where they feel worthless and threatened. Our brains are prediction machines and like certainty. As managers, we are driven to change things in order to improve performance, so we talk a lot about the need for change.

FIGURE 33.2 How managers impact worthiness

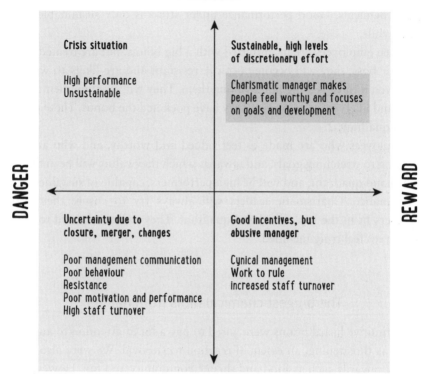

The idea of change, with all the uncertainty that brings, triggers all the wrong brain chemicals and therefore all the wrong behaviours.

A manager who recognizes the individual contributions of people, and who encourages good communication and teamwork, will be helping to induce the right neurotransmitters. When you feel pride in something you've done, and you feel valued, you are experiencing the effects of serotonin, which regulates happiness and anxiety. In addition, when you feel that you belong, and you trust the people around you, you are experiencing the effects of oxytocin. (This neurotransmitter is sometimes called the trust drug. It occurs especially when someone recognizes something we have done or demonstrates a personal touch with us.) So, if you behave in a way that will induce serotonin and oxytocin in your team, you make sure that everyone wants to perform well so they can experience positive, generous and support-ive moments. It is addictive. It is the classic virtuous circle.

If, however, a manager promotes an ultra-competitive, performance-driven culture that puts winning at any cost ahead of teamwork and collaboration, they will be promoting endorphins and dopamine. However, they will also be inducing a chemical that is damaging, called cortisol. This is the neurochemical activated by stress, our so-called fight or flight response. If your team lacks trust, and constantly faces the threat of being beaten or shown up, everyone will experience the negative effects of cortisol. This neurochemical doesn't subside as quickly as the others and levels of cortisol can quickly build up, leaving us in a constant state of anxiety and fear, which can lead to depression and loss of motivation in the workplace. That will also induce insomnia, which will only exacerbate poor performance.

NINE KEY NEUROTRANSMITTERS

These are the nine neurotransmitters worth understanding a little better. The first four – dopamine, serotonin, endorphins and oxytocin – are the ones leaders ought to be working hardest to induce in members of their teams.

Dopamine – associated with feelings of pleasure and satisfaction. It plays a role in the brain's reward system, helping reinforce behaviours that result in reward. Dopamine also helps to aid the flow of information to the brain regions responsible for thought and emotion. *Leaders can encourage dopamine by recognizing when people have successfully completed tasks, by giving praise and by recognizing employees for their ideas and efforts.*

Serotonin – contributes to feelings of well-being and happiness. It impacts every part of your body, from your emotions to your motor skills, and is considered a natural mood stabilizer. It also helps with sleeping, eating and digestion. Appropriate levels of serotonin help to reduce depression, regulate anxiety and even heal wounds. *Serotonin is induced when leaders show they care for their employees, or when they enable high levels of trust in a team. When employees are made to feel confident, their serotonin levels will be higher.*

Endorphins – released in the brain during exercise, excitement, pain and sexual activity, producing feelings of well-being or even euphoria. The principal function of endorphins is to inhibit the communication of pain signals. *Leaders who make work a place where employees have a sense of fun, where they can laugh and where they are being stretched, will help to create the right levels of endorphin, which will encourage repeat behaviour.*

Oxytocin – this is a powerful hormone that influences social interaction. When people hug or kiss a loved one, levels of oxytocin increase, thus it is often called 'the love hormone'. It is also the neurotransmitter that underlies individual and social trust and is crucial to teamwork and collaboration. *Leaders who can create among employees a sense of belonging, of community, connection and collaboration, will stimulate oxytocin. Showing empathy, appreciation, smiling, a good handshake – all these are good for oxytocin levels.*

Adrenaline – produced in high stress or exciting situations, crucial to the body's fight or flight response, but overexposure can be damaging to health. Adrenaline causes a noticeable increase in strength and performance, as well as heightened awareness. This is how injured people can continue to operate when in danger, even when in pain. However, when we perceive a threat that presents no real life-threatening danger, adrenaline can leave people feeling restless and irritable, and can cause heart damage, insomnia and a jittery, nervous feeling. *Creating just the right level of stress, so that employees are out of their comfort zone but not feeling in danger, is what leaders need to achieve. This will create appropriate levels of adrenaline, where too much stress, especially for too long, will create harmful levels.*

Noradrenaline –referred to as a stress hormone which triggers our fight or flight response. In order to make our bodies work as efficiently as possible, noradrenaline increases the amount of oxygen going to our brain to help us think clearer and faster. It increases our heart rate, which pumps more blood around the body to help our muscles work faster and more efficiently. It increases glucose, which gives our muscles something to feed on. It increases our breathing rate to enable more oxygen for the body and the brain. However, it also raises blood pressure.

GABA – a major inhibitory neurotransmitter. Its role is to calm firing nerves in the central nervous system. This in turn has a broad range of effects on the body and mind, including increased relaxation, reduced stress, a more calm and balanced mood, alleviation of pain and a boost to sleep.

Acetylcholine – the principal neurotransmitter involved in thought, learning and memory. It also plays a major part in the autonomic nervous system and works to activate muscles,

Glutamate – the most common neurotransmitter in the brain, involved in cognitive functions such as learning and memory. Too much can be toxic. This is an excitatory neurotransmitter, the brain's 'on switch'.

There are many more neurotransmitters and I must warn you that I may have oversimplified the explanation of each of the above. I don't suggest that you have to become an expert in the science of neurotransmitters, but I do think you need to understand that they exist and that they have a major impact on how people feel and behave. I also want you to understand that your behaviours as a leader will have a massive impact on the chemicals in the brains of your followers, sometimes with devastating consequences, as discussed below.

Change triggers the threat response

Change or ambiguity can trigger the threat response in our brains. The resulting neurochemicals will cause distraction and anxiety, possibly even fear. That, in turn, leads to poor decision-making and poor thinking, and increases the chances of anger and hostility. All that can lead to poor performance and more aggressive relationships. All of that, of course, will result in the need for even greater change. With high levels of these neurotransmitters in the brain, team members will have less emotional control, experience narrow vision, a heightened perception of threats, possibly where they don't exist, and will likely see colleagues as more hostile than they really are.

If you can help your team members to feel worthy, supported, part of a strong and transparent culture, with clear goals, and that they are moving towards reward, you put them in the top right-hand quadrant of the diagram and will encourage all the right behaviours. With increased levels of dopamine, noradrenaline, oxytocin and acetylcholine, you're more likely to produce high-performing teams. This is because these neurochemicals will help people feel positive, focused, resilient and more likely to collaborate. They will also be more able to learn quickly, be more open to new ideas and therefore be more innovative and creative.

Managers who don't communicate with their teams, or who show anger when they hear bad news, or who unwittingly convey that they are disinterested in what team members have to say, or who show a lack of sincerity, or who behave in ways that are inconsistent, will be having a powerful negative effect on the brains of their followers. Even those who think they are doing well might be falling into this trap. Managers consistently overrate their performance and are unaware of how poorly their followers see them. We will see in Chapter 36 that there is a huge gap between how employees rate the behaviours of managers, and how managers rate themselves. Even the most well-intentioned managers may be having a negative effect.

How charismatic leaders create positive behaviours

Leaders with the skills of charisma will help to induce a brain-friendly environment, a factory for the right neurochemicals that encourage positive behaviours. Those who genuinely behave in the right ways are able to increase the levels of motivation, discretionary effort and performance – all because they are creating an environment in which the team wants to perform well.

Authenticity helps the brain and builds trust ✅

With an authentic personality, a leader communicates and lives a strong set of personal values. This makes that leader more predictable and encourages feelings of integrity and fairness. These appeal to our basic survival instinct, because in our primitive brains it is all about having a fair share of food and warmth from the fire. When leaders are inconsistent, or show favouritism to one person and not another, or appear insincere and unpredictable, they set up uncertainty in our brains, which in turn induces the neurochemicals we least want. Most importantly, an authentic manager will engender trust, and encourage trust among members of the team – and trust has a powerful positive effect on our brains.

People with personal power provide confidence ⚡

Having personal power is all about confidence. When leaders project confidence and help people to feel calm and focused, positive and optimistic, they again have a positive influence on our brain chemicals. That confidence and focus helps to create alignment among members of the team and fosters good relationships. The emotional state of leaders is like a contagion that affects all of those around them, even when leaders are trying their best to hide the negative emotions. Leaders with confidence are easily able to engage with people, fostering good working relationships.

Warm leaders make people feel good and perform well ☀

Leaders have a positive affective presence when they are good listeners and encourage their followers to feel that they have a voice in what happens. They are also skilled at making people feel important and worthy, because they are appreciative and praiseful and they encourage a strong sense of self-esteem.

All of this enables autonomy and self-direction. We all have a deep-seated need for a sense of control, or else we are made to feel helpless and therefore unlikely to survive. This is why a sense of autonomy is so important. A lack of autonomy is threatening. Employees with autonomy believe their initiative and engagement will influence the course of events at the company, and this is the very essence of creativity and commitment. Leaders with a strong affective presence are also focused on building relationships. They make members of the team feel that they are connected and aligned with others, safe with the team. Effective leaders are inclusive and strengthen diversity and integrate points of view from different genders, ages and philosophies while always encouraging an environment of respect. By building this emotional capital and the levels of trust and security, they encourage cooperation and collaboration.

Drive and purpose provide certainty and direction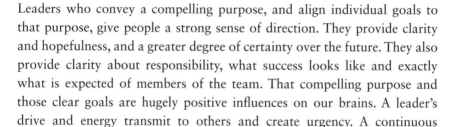

Leaders who convey a compelling purpose, and align individual goals to that purpose, give people a strong sense of direction. They provide clarity and hopefulness, and a greater degree of certainty over the future. They also provide clarity about responsibility, what success looks like and exactly what is expected of members of the team. That compelling purpose and those clear goals are hugely positive influences on our brains. A leader's drive and energy transmit to others and create urgency. A continuous improvement culture enables agility and innovation because it creates a safe place to admit mistakes and correct them, at speed.

Persuasive leaders provide clarity and conviction

Persuasive leaders know that words can change your brain chemistry. They take care when choosing their words. Positive language can transform our reality and encourage high levels of motivation. Positive words propel the motivational centres of the brain into action and build resilience. Negative words have precisely the opposite effect. For example, the word NO floods the brain with stress-producing hormones which impair logic, reason, language processing and communication. Persuasive leaders think carefully about what to say, how to say it and when to say it to achieve maximum effect. Persuasive leaders also know that stories have a powerful positive effect on our brains. We have a strong need to understand and comprehend others, and storytelling provides a pathway for people to step into the shoes of others and see the world as they see it. Stories cut through to our emotions and deliver messages directly to our hearts.

An exclusive focus on numbers shuts down the brain

Too often, managers who lack the skills of charisma will focus only on financial metrics and the dashboard measures of desired performance. This is the wrong place to start, and brain science now tells us that doing so can cause people to shut down cognitively, emotionally and perceptually. To get people to open up their minds, you need to discuss the purpose of an activity, and relate it to the goals of the organization. Once people understand the why, they can better relate to the metrics.

Charismatic leaders never forget to take time to understand what really motivates people. When charismatic leaders create positive chemical factories in the brains of their followers, everyone will benefit. Customers will receive better service and products; employees will be happier, healthier and more productive; teams will be more creative, collaborative and become higher performing; the leaders will achieve their goals – and shareholders will be delighted.

34

Why charisma is essential in a digital world

We need a new kind a leader for a new age of rapid change, as the technology revolution forces us to rethink the role of humans in the workplace. Employees at every level in companies will have to become more adept at change, and that means being willing to learn, and relearn, and discover and learn over and over again, as the world keeps evolving around them. Leaders will need to have the right skills to enable and encourage this change. They will need to promote creativity and innovation at a pace never achieved before.

Advances in technology have revolutionized our lives over the past 10 years, at a rate that is unprecedented in human history. If we think that has all happened quickly, hold on to your hats, because the pace of change is only going to speed up. The sheer scale, velocity and complexity of what we now call the Fourth Industrial Revolution is ensuring that whatever we think is fast today will be pedestrian by tomorrow. We are experiencing a tsunami of change, which will fundamentally transform the way we live, the way we work and the way we relate to each other.

The First Industrial Revolution was fuelled by iron and steam engines. The second was powered by electricity, steel, chemicals and telecommunications. The Third Industrial Revolution ushered in the information age with world-changing innovations in computing, the internet, mobile communications and more. The Fourth Industrial Revolution is based on innovation driven by combinations of technologies and billions upon billions of connections. It is disrupting every company, every industry, in every corner of the globe.

This fusion of technologies is enabling connections in ways we never imagined before. When you connect billions of people and things through mobile devices with huge computing power, the possibilities are unlimited. Now add to all this the constantly evolving technology in fields such as artificial intelligence, robotics, the internet of things, quantum computing, biotechnology and materials science, and I think you will understand why I use the phrase 'a tsunami of change'.

Massive changes to society and work

When combined, these technologies will drive massive changes to individual lives as well as societies, workforces and economies.

While the first two revolutions powered massive improvements in productivity, ironically, productivity today has sunk to one-third the rate of the previous 100 years. This is why many people are talking about how the Fourth Industrial Revolution will bring massive job losses. There is a huge drive to improve productivity through more automation, which will displace jobs.

A McKinsey Global Institute report on *The Future of the Workforce* suggests that up to 375 million people globally will have to change their occupation and acquire new skills by the year 2030. Research from Gartner, a global research and consulting business, suggests that 90 per cent of the jobs we are familiar with today will be replaced by smart machines by 2030.

Of the children entering school today, it is forecast that something like 70 per cent will assume careers that don't even exist yet. Like what? I hear you ask. Imagine roles like a space tour guide, or a medical roboticist. What about an augmented reality architect or an avatar relationship manager? How about a drone dispatcher, or a nano-weapons specialist? These ideas are not too far-fetched. After all, if there is an increase in the number of medical robots, who will service them? If more and more parcels are to be delivered by drones to our homes, who will manage them?

In addition, technology will enable a more service-based and remote-working culture. For example, trained nurses could be freed to relieve the pressure on doctors by going out to people's homes more, armed with the data they need to provide health services at the patient's bedside. New technologies are enabling more remote-working, or co-working spaces and teleconferencing. Organizations are likely to have an ever-smaller pool of core full-time employees for fixed functions, backed up by colleagues in other countries and external consultants and contractors for specific projects. There will be a far greater emphasis on collaborating with other companies to provide joined-up services to customers.

People are now working more fluidly across traditional departmental boundaries, in order to get projects completed more quickly. In order to be more agile, organizations are having to adopt a swarm-based work ethic that allows people quickly to assemble around shared goals and then disperse just as speedily. Maintaining rigid institutions and hierarchies is therefore becoming harder to justify, and organizations are increasingly trying to flatten their hierarchies to speed up decision-making and reduce costs.

A new kind of manager for a new age

The point is that this fourth revolution is moving at an exponential rather than a linear pace. Because it is disrupting almost every industry, in every country, it also means that managers need to transform. We need a new kind a leader for this new age of rapid change. Managers will need to think about how to play a central role in enabling this, and turning their organizations into customer-obsessed, innovation powerhouses. This technology revolution is going to force us to fundamentally rethink the role of humans in the workplace and enable them to move into a territory that robots can't occupy – creativity. This is where humans will focus – creating new value – given that robots will take the drudgery out of daily work and give them the tools and space to be more creative.

Each year, the World Economic Forum (WEF) publishes its *Future of Jobs Report*, available on its website. It forecasts the top 10 job skills required for workers to thrive in the next year, according to global chief human resources officers. As a benchmark, they show what people thought those skills would need to be for 2015. Compared side by side, the shifts we will experience in 2020 aren't too dramatic – except for one skill.

1. THE TOP 10 SKILLS IN 2015 WERE:

1 complex problem-solving;

2 coordinating with others;

3 people management;

4 critical thinking;

   5 negotiation;

   6 quality control;

   7 service orientation;

   8 judgement and decision-making;

   9 active listening;

   10 *creativity*.

2. THE TOP 10 SKILLS FOR 2020 WERE:

   1 complex problem-solving;

   2 critical thinking;

   3 *creativity;*

   4 people management;

   5 coordinating with others;

   6 emotional intelligence;

   7 judgement and decision-making;

   8 service orientation;

   9 negotiation;

   10 cognitive flexibility.

Did you spot the rise of creativity? Yes, *creativity,* which is even above emotional intelligence. Notice it made a big jump from the no. 10 spot all the way up to no. 3. By creativity, they don't mean artistic creativity reserved for designers, writers or musicians. They mean the ability to think in ways that solve problems, generate ideas or improve processes and products.

   For certain, employees at every level in companies will have to become adept at change, and that means being willing to learn, and relearn, and discover and learn over and over again, as the world keeps evolving around them. And managers will need to have the right skills to enable this change. Leadership is all about change. If there is no need for change, there is no need for leaders. But in a world of such rapid change, there has never been a greater need for charismatic leadership. The pace of a leader determines the pace of the pack, so leaders everywhere have to upgrade their skills of change management and recognize that they have to turbo-charge their ability to lead their teams in the right direction, at the right speed.

Neither employees nor managers have prepared adequately for the shift that is already underway. Findings of *The Workforce 2020* study conducted by Oxford Economics underscore this. The report, based on a survey of more than 2,700 executives and 2,700 employees, in 27 countries, found that problems with talent and key skills are already affecting business performance. Half of the employees say they do not expect their current skills to be adequate in just three years from now. These concerns are exacerbated by a sense from most of those interviewed that fewer than half work at companies that have 'a culture of continuous learning'.

For all these reasons, there is a growing demand for soft skills in organizations, not only because these skills are intrinsically necessary, but also because they are vital to help employees learn and develop for what will be ever-changing new responsibilities. Those soft skills are increasingly difficult to find in job applicants.

Soft skills are a business imperative

As the nature of work is disrupted, soft skills are now a business imperative. Leaders will not only have to have exceptional soft skills themselves; they will also have to be able to cultivate soft skills throughout their enterprises. Traditional hierarchies are going to flatten and leadership will be required everywhere to help drive companies forward. Those organizations that do develop soft skill programmes will be able to identify and cultivate formal and informal leaders everywhere. Those who show talent in building teams, fostering creativity and problem-solving, and facilitating adaptability, will be those able to provide the best solutions. They will also be able to be role models for colleagues who struggle in developing these essential soft skills. This kind of manager will have immense curiosity and will constantly be proactively seeking a better way to do business for the sake of their company and their teams.

Business forecasters are now suggesting that workforces will soon be split into two basic groups: the first being more technology-focused people carrying out the technical jobs necessary in a more digitally advanced workplace; and the second group being more charismatic, innovative individuals who will be leading the changes and developing the relationships that enable success. Robots will not be able to deal with unique problems, which is where humans come into their own. This is why we need to develop these skills even further and be happy to leave mechanical, mundane tasks to artificial intelligence and robots.

Being able to innovate at speed will be an essential skill of management, which will bring teamwork and collaboration, problem-solving and critical thinking, communication and relationships right to the fore. Managers who can influence and facilitate employees to bring out their creative skills will be in high demand. To drive success, managers will have to unleash all of the talent within their organization and then use it to its full potential. Business leaders are seeking creative, adaptive managers who will unlock innovation, delivering big ideas that lead to better services that help them serve their customers better.

Improving drive and motivation is essential to success

First and foremost, this requires managers to design and implement actions aimed at boosting their team's motivation and engagement. Managers must have the skills to handle this pace of change, especially when they may have to lead people who don't work in the same office or the same country or even necessarily on the same day. At a time when they will be facing unprecedented pressure to perform, to become simultaneously more cost-effective and more innovative, while dealing with huge levels of uncertainty and complexity, managers will have to put themselves between the chaos of change and their people. To do so effectively, will require managers to ensure they are skilled in all five key traits of charisma:

- Managers with authentic personalities will be able to build the levels of trust that are essential to good teamwork and collaboration. Without teamwork and collaboration, there can be little innovation. Without innovation, companies will quickly fall behind their competitors.

- Managers with the right personal power will be able to infuse their teams with positivity and confidence and will be oriented to action. They will be problem-solvers able to call on the diverse skills and viewpoints of their team members to create the best solutions.

- Those with an affective presence will be able to create a sense of worth and belonging, at a time of huge uncertainty. Most importantly they will also be able to make employees feel safe at a time of enormous disruption. Having a sense of worth, as we have seen, is one of the most important needs of employees and drives high levels of discretionary effort.

- Managers who are able to convey a compelling purpose and connect their teams to it will keep their employees relentlessly focused on customers, and thus focused on rapid and continuous improvement.
- Managers with the charismatic skill of persuasiveness will connect people to the cause and their communication skills will enable the conversations that will drive new ideas and keep essential relationships in good order.

The time has come for all managers to understand that these soft skills of charisma will determine their success in business, more so than the technical skills that probably got them into a leadership position in the first place. (Research conducted with Fortune 500 CEOs by the Stanford Research Institute International and the Carnegie Melon Foundation found that 75 per cent of long-term job success depends on people skills, while only 25 per cent on technical knowledge.)

In an era of unprecedented disruption and change, we've never needed charismatic leaders more.

35

The dark side of charisma

Charisma without ethics can lead to dangerous and dark places. Charisma without the other essential skills of management can lead to influential but ineffective and possibly even harmful managers. To be effective, managers need balanced charisma.

We all know of charismatic people who were evil or warped. Ask anyone to name someone who was charismatic but murderous, or charismatic but evil, or even charismatic but demonic, and you'll quickly get answers. A demonic charismatic would be Charles Manson. An evil charismatic would be Adolf Hitler. A murderous charismatic would be serial killer Ted Bundy. The list goes on an on – from political leaders like Stalin or Idi Amin, to cult leaders like Jim Jones or David Koresh, both of whom led their followers to mass suicides.

So, there can be no doubt that charisma does have a dark side. In the cases of the people I have cited above, the malevolent impact of their charisma was plain for the world to see. In organizations, however, the negative impact of charisma can be more subtle, but still destructive and dangerous.

For example, leaders who stand on a stage and thrill an audience with great storytelling, a keen wit and an amazing grasp of facts, will entrance us. We say they are great communicators. But are they? If they step off the stage and cannot or will not listen to followers, or cannot (or worse, will not) facilitate open and robust debate among team members and other stakeholders, then they are committed only to one-way communication, and that can be hugely destructive. A leader who won't listen could be doing so to avoid challenge so that they can pursue a personal agenda. Or because they believe arrogantly that they are right and no one else could possibly have a valid point of view. Either way, the result will be dangerous, to both business effectiveness and employee morale.

Strong charismatics can dominate teams

When a leader with charisma becomes so strong and confident that they dominate their teams to the extent that others simply never question their decisions, you'd better hope that that leader is always right and is leading you in the right direction. Sadly, the opposite is usually true. Leaders who cut themselves off from bad news or challenge, quickly lose sight of the real drivers of success, or the drivers of failure, and a slow and tortured decline usually ensues. They even become blind to the dangers facing them, personally, because of excessive confidence.

Diverse views, born of genuine diversity in the team, are key to agility and innovation, which are more critical in an age of rapid change. If a charismatic leader uses their charisma in the wrong way, they might encourage team members to think that disagreement is disloyalty. Leaders who use charisma in the right way will encourage team members to speak up, in the knowledge that this serves two useful purposes. First, it is most likely the best way to improve outcomes for the team. Second, it will help people to feel valued and keep their levels of motivation high.

Blind followers who are loyal to their charismatic leader will almost certainly lead to poor decision-making, and even allow for unethical behaviour by the leader. Too much charisma can dilute good judgement, because it can be based on emotional manipulation, which disallows more rationale points of view, or causes people to keep quiet when they know they should be speaking up.

Glib charm can make people think that some leaders are charismatic, and this can hide their worst tendencies. Being highly manipulative, or hugely egocentric, might not sound like terrible sins, but they are when put to the wrong purpose. Charismatic leaders who are well-balanced can inspire us to work together for a common cause, they can create a great sense of team among high-performing individuals, and they can enable huge levels of agility and creativity by fostering trust and dialogue.

At their worst, charismatic leaders – bereft of humility – may develop tunnel vision and cut themselves off from what matters most in their organization. They will be unwilling to learn from their mistakes and become unresponsive to team members or other stakeholders. There's always a danger that charismatic leaders who lack ethics could be committing all kinds of violations. Team members may turn a blind eye and fail to report transgressions. Even when things are going well, if a charismatic manager leaves, this can be hugely disruptive to the team. Overdependence on a leader can inhibit the development of a competent successor.

Charisma alone is not enough

Charisma without ethics can lead us to dangerous and dark places, at worst, and charisma without the other essential skills of management can lead to us being seen as inefficient as managers, with good cause. The dark side of charisma is about a lack of balance, both in the skills of charisma, and in a lack of other essential management skills. Most of these skills are essential soft skills, and, most organizations are sadly doing too little to help us develop those skills. It is up to us as individuals to take the initiative and educate ourselves.

Of course, charisma alone is not enough to be a good leader. There are plenty of other skills that you need in management and leadership to complement the skills of charisma. If you can improve your charismatic presence, you will be far more likely to motivate others and encourage high levels of discretionary effort from them. This, of course, is one of the primary tasks of a manager – to achieve critical goals through the efforts of others. However, you still need to be able to do strategic planning, understand budgets, be a good coach and a brilliant project manager.

For my previous books on leadership, I was fortunate to interview 120 CEOs. After every interview, I asked them what they were looking for when they were hiring leaders into their own organizations. The answers were consistent. Most often mentioned, in order of priority, they were looking for:

1 raw intellect and the ability to analyse and solve problems, and to think strategically, and with clarity;

2 the ability to choose the right people, making sure they had the best of the best on their teams;

3 the ability to inspire people and align them to a cause;

4 a good communicator, a good listener;

5 a strong sense of mission;

6 integrity, authenticity, strong values, honesty, openness and curiosity;

7 domain excellence (knowledge and experience of the business they lead); and of course

8 numeracy, and a focus on performance and results.

Notice that domain skills – the specialized skills of the field in which you operate – came only seventh on the list. Other skills they looked for included:

Self-organization and delegation. Management is often a very lonely, complex, fraught and demanding job where you have to juggle many different responsibilities and goals. Being able to manage your own workload as well as delegate effectively to employees is crucial to your success and even your sanity.

Forward planning and strategic thinking. As a manager you have to think long-term while simultaneously focusing on today's tasks and responsibilities. Leadership is that which you do to create a different future, and management is that which you do to ensure you're doing the right things in the right way today.

Commercial awareness. A good manager has to have high levels of numeracy and an ability to set high standards and deliver the team performance that delivers the right results. Understanding the marketplace, and what makes the business successful, and making sure that customers were served profitably, was a key skill.

Solving complex problems and making decisions. As a manager, you have to be brilliant at solving problems every single day. And that means using the diverse views of your team to define and solve problems faster.

Coaching. Being a good coach is a prerequisite if you want to be seen by your bosses as a good manager.

New media and new data literacy. The ability to access, analyse, evaluate and create relevant data will be a key part of being an effective manager. Equally, as teams become more spread out, operating remotely from different locations and different countries, managers will need to be able to use technology to communicate and collaborate. This kind of virtual collaboration through online devices will be key to driving engagement and increasing productivity.

Bad managers kill companies

Bad managers kill potential and slaughter performance. They are not bad people, but they are bad leaders. Some are so bad they are like energy vampires, sucking the dedication and motivation right out of us. They became managers because they had great technical skills and did the job better than the rest of us, but now, as a leader, they are clueless.

Because of bad bosses, we find it really hard to get motivated. We turn up for work and do the bare minimum to stay in the job. In any case, we don't really understand what we have to do, or what 'good' looks like. We get little in the way of constructive feedback or recognition, so we don't feel great about ourselves. We don't feel like we are a member of a team, and the team anyway feels dysfunctional and competitive – distinctly *not* a team. We really don't feel we know who this manager is or why they want us to do the things they ask of us. They feel ineffectual when in front of us, without substance, and they can't string two words together coherently. Worse, they seem to have no idea how their behaviours affect us.

This kind of manager makes us want to leave. It's a great company, and we love what this company does, but anything would be better than this job – and so we polish up our CVs, read the job smalls, speak to head-hunters, and before long, we move somewhere else. (There is a horrible HR truth that haunts most companies and it is this: employees who rate their direct manager's performance poorly, are *four* times as likely to be job hunting.)

Do you recognize this state of affairs? How do you rate your manager? If you are a manager, what chance this might be you? Sadly, the odds are quite high that the answer is yes to all these questions, and in the case of the final question, I'm afraid the answer is more than 50 per cent. The Chartered Management Institute (CMI), a UK chartered management body dedicated to raising the standards of management and leadership, says that as many as four out of five managers in the UK are what they call 'accidental managers' – managers who have been promoted to their role without adequate training. In the UK alone, that's an estimated 2.4 million bosses who are highly likely to suck at their jobs. Imagine how many employees that may affect? The Chartered Institute of Personnel Development estimates that less than half of all employees are satisfied with their manager. The World Bank estimates there are 3.4 billion workers around the world. How many of them are feeling disengaged and demotivated? This brings with it a massive cost in lost productivity.

How to be the opposite of charismatic

To my mind, the opposite of charisma is repulsiveness. If charisma is about attracting and inspiring, then anti-charisma must be about repelling people, and being obnoxious and offensive. However, in the context of this book, we are talking about what makes a really good manager vs what makes a bad one, based on their charisma.

There are people who are appropriately charismatic, but who lack the ability to problem-solve, or develop a strategy, or don't know enough about the technical aspects of the job that their team is required to do, and lacking these skills may negatively impact on their effectiveness as a leader. However, with the right charismatic skills, such a leader would still be able to draw on the knowledge and expertise of others to cover those shortfalls. Those who lack many of the skills of charisma may be making some dreadful mistakes, often unintentionally, but nevertheless with the same devastating consequences.

On the basis that knowing what *not* to do can be just as helpful as knowing what's right, I offer the following checklist to help you be more aware of the bad behaviours which will make you disliked, ineffective and possibly even likely soon to be fired. There are some leaders who simply don't care about others and it is this level of disregard that leads them to be really bad bosses. They create truly toxic places to work, and so long as they get done what they want done, nothing else matters.

On the other hand, there are also managers (far greater in number) who are well-intentioned and who do care about people, but who simply lack the skills to do a better job of encouraging discretionary effort. A lack of awareness about what really matters to people leads them to be bad bosses to work for, even though they are likely to be far less toxic and also likely to want to improve.

As you read this list of bad behaviours, reflect for a moment on each point and consider whether you may be guilty of this sin, to some degree or other. Be tough on yourself, because your employees most certainly will be. Examine whether you may be unmindful of any of these sins and may therefore inadvertently be guilty of bad behaviour.

Bad behaviours that destroy authenticity and trust 🎯

1 The very worst kind of boss to work for is one who lacks integrity or displays integrity inconsistently. Those with integrity stay true to their values and are prepared to make tough choices about what's right rather than what's convenient. When you get to a place where integrity plays no part in your management, no one can trust you. Without a moral compass and ethics, or even just a sense of what's fair, the team will quickly dissolve into bad behaviours and poor performance, based on a lack of trust of their leader. This trust deficit floods into their daily working life and infects their relationships with all of their teammates. Even when leaders

do have integrity, their employees often see it differently. This is because their employees will observe inconsistent behaviours from their bosses which, while simply thoughtless, will lead them to make judgements about the character of their boss. Equally, such inconsistencies, or even the want of speaking up on issues, can make a boss seem insincere and dishonest. Leadership is an act of courage and being courageous often means standing up for the things you truly believe in, even in the most difficult of circumstances. Those without integrity will stand up for very little, and hypocrisy quickly follows.

2   Bad bosses discriminate amongst members of their team. They have favourites, whom they shield from the effects of doing shoddy work, or with whom they favour good assignments or great working hours and shifts. They will expect loyalty but won't be loyal themselves. They divide and conquer, and set up discord in the team, by favouring the opinion of some over others. Members of the team will quickly notice this and then distrust, disengagement and demotivation quickly follow.

3   Bosses who trust no one are toxic. Distrustful managers will tend to micromanage others, check everything that people are doing, or disbelieve people unless they can conclusively prove their point of view. This lack of trust will lead to massive bottlenecks. Bottlenecks lead to a loss of productivity. A micromanager will seldom delegate. They ask to be copied in on every e-mail, will want to go to every meeting and will make every decision and solve every problem. They will then make a really big deal out of working 80 hours a week. They care little that that team members feel disenchanted and disempowered. In fact, this actually creates a vicious circle, because if they do sense this disengagement, they will be even less likely to delegate.

4   Leaders who keep themselves to themselves can be very damaging to team morale. Those who never speak up for the values they believe in and make it very difficult for people to read them, set up a wariness among their employees, which also leads to a lack of trust. Any employee who finds their boss aloof and doesn't really know where their boss is coming from will regard them as dangerous and unpredictable.

5   Managers who lack self-awareness or humility are damaging. When leaders think they are, for example, great communicators, and members of the team think otherwise, credibility suffers. On the other hand, leaders who show vulnerability are often perceived to be more effective as leaders, because they show more of their human side. As tough as it is to admit

mistakes, humility is one of the most powerful attributes of managers and is a great accelerator of building trust.

Ways to destroy your personal power 🖋

6 A love of politics destroys relationships. Bad managers love politics, suck up to their own bosses and especially favour those who suck up to them.

7 Use fear and bureaucracy as tools to manage. Poor managers would never consider liberating people to have more autonomy. They want employees to feel lucky that they've got a job and always hand over assignments with the threat that if it isn't delivered the way they would like it, there will be highly negative consequences. 'It's my way or the highway', they say. They use disciplinary measures when simply communicating with an employee would get the desired result. Because they are bullies, they will tolerate bullying in the team. Such fear-based management may get short-term results but is simply unsustainable.

8 Make promises to employees, and then break them. Even if they have the intention to do something, and then forget, this will result in a lack of trust from employees.

9 Ride authority for all it's worth. Poor managers expect others to serve them and serve their egos. They'll never roll their sleeves up and will ensure that others do the jobs that they are no longer willing to do themselves. Humble leaders are often out in front, leading by doing and by example. Bad bosses try to promote themselves at the cost of the team, always playing for themselves, at every opportunity. They will take credit for others work.

10 Don't worry about standards, and don't care about quality or delivering projects on time.

11 Never apologize, and never accept responsibility for mistakes. With bad managers, it will always be someone else's fault. As for personal development, learning is for losers. And they never learn from mistakes; because they don't make them.

12 Constantly brag about their exploits and so-called achievements. Also, constantly demonstrate high intellect, thus belittling and demeaning those who follow you.

13 Panic under pressure, and let it show. Bad managers rush around and overreact to even the smallest problems, often causing despair and disdain in equal measure.

14 Be negative about their own bosses, blaming them for everything that's wrong about the organization. Bad bosses never accept that they have the ability to change anything themselves.

Managers without warmth make employees disengage

15 Bad listeners are often bad managers, and worse, they either don't care or are simply unaware of that fact. They regularly show employees that they have no interest in their input and perspectives and treat their views with contempt or disdain.

16 Managers who show little empathy or compassion for members of their team will also have a hugely negative effect on morale and engagement.

17 Highly critical and vocal managers will seldom celebrate successes, and will relentlessly and publicly interrogate failures, never forgiving mistakes. They never offer second chances and can see no value in giving the benefit of the doubt to others. They will constantly search for faults in employees and ignore their strengths. This kind of behaviour will make every new assignment, and every member of the team, feel very unsafe.

18 Bad managers are disrespectful of everyone. They show contempt for their employees, their own bosses and even their customers. Disrespect is contagious, and very soon members of the team will be disrespecting each other and disrespecting customers too, with disastrous consequences.

19 Bad managers lack any charm and are cold and aloof. They are not interested in building relationships. They have no interest in the motivations and personal lives of their team members. They pay little attention to work–life balance, and their team members are constantly overworked, with a high risk of burnout.

20 Worst of all, bad managers are not inclusive. They exclude people from critical conversations. They have little tolerance for diversity. They prefer 'birds of a feather' in their team and are not interested in teams that are built on a diversity of gender, race, culture or nationality. Even if they have strongly diverse teams, bad managers make little effort to ensure that everyone is included in team discussions or decisions.

Without cause or drive, managers destroy a sense of purpose

21 Bad managers are never clear about their expectations, timelines or goals. Worse, they change their minds frequently and leave team members feeling off-balance and insecure. If goals look like they are being met, they'll quickly ramp them up to higher, unachievable levels. They are myopically focused on results.

22 They never bother to connect with what the team is doing, to the organization's mission and goals. It always feels as if the team is acting in isolation from the rest of the company, and that there is no meaning or purpose behind what they are doing. The team will feel like they are pursuing pointless goals and also feel disconnected from their colleagues.

23 They will often give the same work to different people, causing confusion about roles and responsibilities, leaving everyone unclear about what exactly they're supposed to be doing.

24 They pay no attention to company or team culture, and certainly don't live up to the values of the workplace themselves.

25 They do nothing about poor-performing or toxic members of staff and will show little interest in constant continuous improvement. They will equally be disinterested in helping employees to grow and develop, regarding this as a waste of time rather than a way to help improve performance.

26 They will show no hesitation in ripping off customers and suppliers at every opportunity, as anything is acceptable in the pursuit of achieving profits.

27 They are not in the least bit interested in how their customers feel.

Poor persuaders kill conversations and innovation ➡

28 Bad managers are secretive and share as little information as possible. Information is power, so they deliberately choose to withhold it.

29 Bad managers are bad at giving feedback. Worse still, bad managers are even worse at giving praise. Employees always see managers who give praise often and appropriately as more effective.

30 With bad managers, one-way communication is rampant. They are on the broadcast button all the time and have no interest in listening to people's views or encouraging robust conversations to find ideal solutions. They care little about encouraging good communication between team members.

31 Bad managers are invisible. They prefer the security of their office walls to going out to talk to members of their team. They send e-mails at all hours of the day and night, even if members of their team are but yards away in the office.

32 Bad managers never prepare for presentations, preferring to speak off the cuff. They have no sense of their audience and are completely unaware of the audience's issues and concerns. They have a message to deliver and, by heck, deliver it they will, no matter how long it takes. They can be ambiguous, indirect or even lie, and never check whether people have understood a single word they said.

Who of us would want to be working in a team led by a boss who exhibits any of the behaviours I have listed above? These are toxic bosses and they create dreadful cultures and poisonous places of work that are harmful to our health, and our ability to contribute meaningfully to our organization. These are the bosses who will have high churn rates in their teams, with most of their employees looking to move to another department or even another company.

Happily, well-intended managers who truly want to improve their performance can address most of these bad behaviours. Being mindful of these destructive behaviours is a good place to start. Even better, in the next chapter we look at how to grade your charisma and understand where you need to focus in order to become more effective.

3 6

What's the shape of *your* charisma?

After testing dozens of leaders on their charisma quotient, I find that we can have significantly different shapes to our charisma. What is the shape of yours? What does it mean? What are the scores that will make you more affective and effective? How can we measure our own charisma, or have others rate us, so that can we can work out how to improve?

There are charismatic leaders who are high on charm and can make us feel as if we are the most important people in their lives, and that they love our ideas and views. They listen well, they charm us and engage with us, they respect us and appreciate us. They find ways to include us and make us feel we belong. They index highly for affective presence and warmth.

There are others whose charisma comes from being passionate about a particular cause, and we are swept up and amazed by their passion and their drive. They have a clear vision, and they show us how we can help, and how our strengths can help them achieve the impossible. Their charisma comes from their cause, and the unwavering passion they have to achieve it.

Other leaders attract us by being hugely transparent, articulate and compelling about the values that drive their behaviours, searingly honest about how they see the world, and themselves. They ooze integrity. They are committed. They attract us because they are so authentic.

Still others can be compelling communicators, who dazzle us with their articulate views. They have a way of connecting with us and relating to us in terms we understand. They focus on issues we are concerned about.

They tell thought-provoking stories that move us to action. They index highly for persuasiveness.

And, finally, there are those who command a room simply by standing in it. Their very presence attracts our attention, because of the way they hold themselves, the way they dress, or the powerful and assertive body language they use. They are always positive, they are optimistic and give us hope, and their energy is contagious. You would give them high marks for personal power.

Some charismatic leaders can be demotivating or toxic

No doubt, each of these types of leader will be seen as charismatic. However, without the other elements of charisma to create the right balance, each of these leaders might also be demotivating, confusing or even toxic. For example, if a person is driven but lacks any ability to make you feel valued or worthwhile, you might find them charismatic, but you certainly wouldn't want to work for them. They would ignore your needs to service their own.

Or, if a leader is driven by a worthy cause, but you feel you can't trust them because they hide who they are and make you suspicious, you'll withhold your commitment, because you'll always be wary of their motives. Once again, this will lead to inhibited performance, which will be extremely difficult to understand and fix.

The key to effective leadership charisma is to have a good balance of all five traits. And the good news for all of us is that, to be effective, we only need to be moderately good in each of the five key elements.

A recent study shows that exceptionally charismatic people are more likely to be bad leaders. Those with moderate levels of charisma, says the research, are more effective at managing an organization. Jasmine Vergauwe, a doctoral student at Ghent University and lead author of the study, published the findings of her research in *The Journal of Personality and Social Psychology* in 2017.

She and her colleagues compared the charisma scores of about 600 business leaders with their effectiveness, as reported by peers, subordinates and superiors. They found that as charisma increased, so did perceived effectiveness, but only up to a point. At a certain level, as charisma scores continued to increase, perceived effectiveness started to decline. 'Leaders with both low and high charismatic personalities were perceived as being less effective than leaders with moderate levels of charisma,' Jasmine reported.

In my own research, detailed more fully later in this chapter, it is clear the leaders are rated highly because of their ability to effect organizational outcomes. It is all about charisma that enables better teams, better relationships, better outcomes and better business results. The key is to have moderately high marks for each of the five traits of charisma.

How different shapes have different effects

In the end, it is all about the shape of your charisma. The diagram in Figure 36.1 shows what a well-balanced charismatic leader would look like. Such a person would have moderately high-level marks on each of the five axes of charisma. This is the shape to aspire to – with a mark of 7 or 8 out of 10 for each trait.

FIGURE 36.1 Balanced charisma

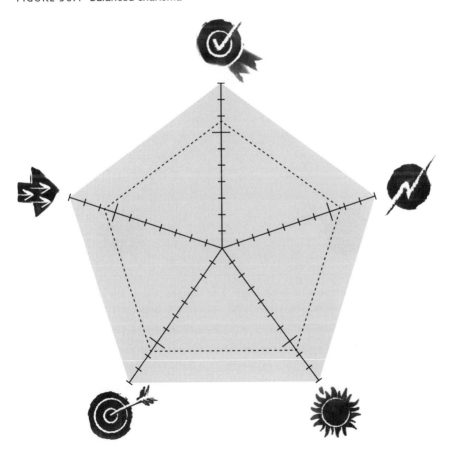

Before we analyse this shape, let us examine warped charisma for a moment. Let us imagine a person who has a high level of authenticity, and a high mark on affective presence (warmth), but low marks on personal power, drive and persuasiveness. Figure 36.2 shows what this shape looks like.

FIGURE 36.2 Warped charisma example (1)

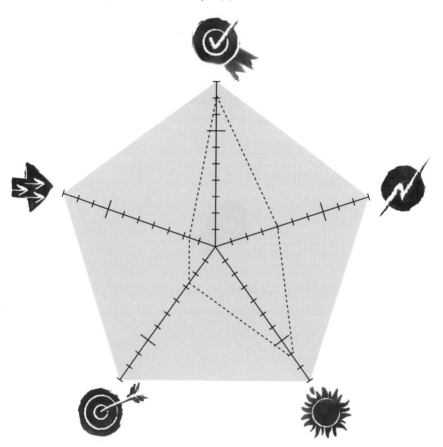

How might that person be perceived? The danger is that they will be seen as a really good person, but hugely ineffective as a leader. Such a person would be seen as transparent and honest, a leader of integrity, who is charming and makes us feel valued and important. The only problem is that they may also be seen as ineffectual, because they lack the ability to give us a sense of direction or focus us on the goals which will get us to our outcomes. They will appreciate team members when they do well or come up with good ideas. However, we may lose respect for them because they lack any strategic direction and because we see them to be personally ineffective. Worse, they will be a poor communicator, and lack persuasiveness, never stating strong points of view on issues.

Now let us look at somebody who gets high marks for authenticity and drive and persuasiveness, but low marks for personal power and warmth (Figure 36.3).

FIGURE 36.3 Warped charisma example (2)

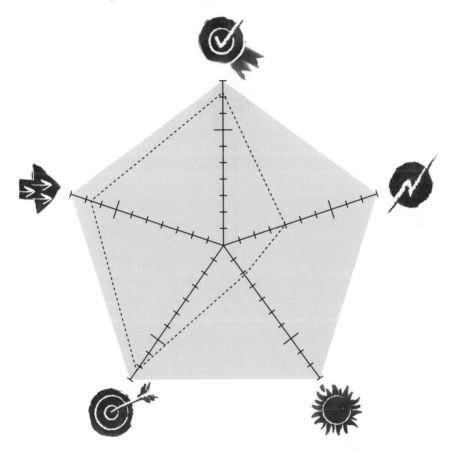

A person with this shape will win our respect, because they will be clear about their own values and seem to be therefore predictable and trustworthy. Furthermore, they will inspire us to a common cause, both because they have real clarity and vision, and because they are highly persuasive. However, they certainly won't make us feel good about ourselves and, lacking empathy, will be unlikely to want to consider our views, praise us or even listen effectively.

They will be unaware of their body language, and may be inclined to negativity and a lack of confidence, all of which will drain our own sense of worth and our own confidence and belief in them.

As you might imagine, there are many different shapes to charisma, and we could examine up to hundred thousand subtle variations. You get the point, so let's do only one more shape by way of example. Let's examine a charismatic leader whose profile is high in authenticity, high in personal power and high in warmth. This person is low in drive and persuasiveness (Figure 36.4).

FIGURE 36.4 Warped charisma example (3)

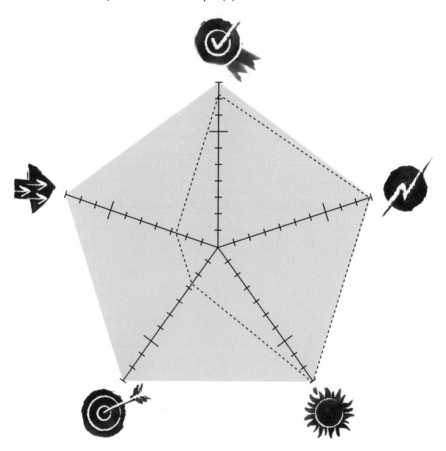

Again, aspects of their charisma will be highly attractive. They will seem to us to be genuine and trustworthy as a leader, they will be poised and confident and carry themselves with gravitas, and they will be highly empathetic, a good listener, appreciative of our efforts. They will make us feel valued, they will make us want to follow them, and they will be able to generate trust and collaboration. However, we will be frustrated by their poor communication skills and confused at their inability to give us a sense of direction and a vision that compels us. They will fail us both in terms of clear long-term goals, and our own daily operational goals. Worse, they are unlikely to be able to connect us to the vision of the organization and give us a sense of meaning and importance. Frustrating!

Well-balanced charisma

Now, let us go back to the shape of a well-balanced charismatic leader, who achieves moderately high marks in each of the skill sets (Figure 36.5). Team members rate them at 6 out of 10 or higher for each of the skill sets.

FIGURE 36.5 Balanced charisma

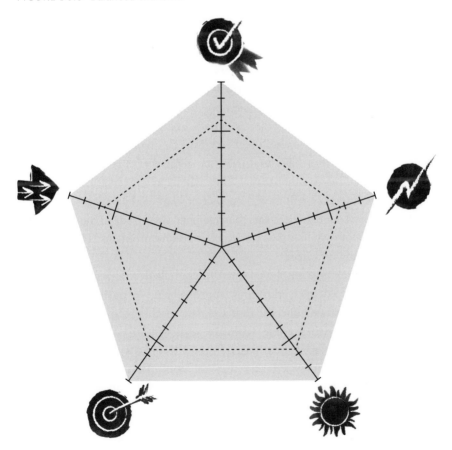

Such a leader would be self-aware enough to know that they have plenty of room for improvement, but they will still be doing a good job in leading the team. Because they are reasonably good at making team members feel valued and appreciated, and because they will listen well and praise appropriately, their employees will be more likely to give of their discretionary effort. They will have a strong presence, and will, most of the time, be positive, energetic and committed. More often than not, they will deliver on their promises and because they are generally open about their own values and passions, will encourage trust and collaboration. They will be doing a good job of connecting the team to the organization's vision and translating that into daily tasks that makes sense. They will also be fairly persuasive, and good at encouraging debate and creativity. They won't be seen as perfect, but they will get a better mark for overall effectiveness than any of the other charismatic shapes I've outlined above.

The business benefits of charisma

These results do matter. The positive effects of charismatic leaders contribute to great performance. When leaders are charismatic, in a balanced way, their employees will trust and be trusted. They will be confident, hopeful and benefit from a sense of positivity about the future. They will feel respected, that they have a voice in what's going on, and will feel valued members of the team. They will feel worthy. They will also have focus, and clarity about what they have to do, and be aligned with the other members of their team, and with other teams. They will be in conversations that drive improvement and they will have a conviction that enables success.

All of this will contribute to their engagement, their pride in their company, and their sense of ownership of company goals and problems. They will give of their discretionary effort.

Global research into employee engagement tells us that improvements in engagement levels deliver enormous improvements in business results, on every key performance indicator that a manager is likely to be measured on. The following statistics come from an organization called Engage for Success, a voluntary movement based in the UK and focused on promoting employee engagement as a better way to work. They studied dozens of companies in the UK and found engagement delivered positive benefits in the following ways:

- **Income growth** – highly engaged workforces saw an average of 13.7 per cent improvement in net income growth. Lower engaged companies saw a decline of 3.8 per cent. Those in the top quartile demonstrated revenue growth 2.5 times greater than those in the bottom quartile.

- **Profit** – companies with engagement scores in the top quartile have twice the annual net profit of those in the bottom quartile.

- **Productivity and performance** – companies with engagement scores in the top quartile average an 18 per cent higher level of productivity than those in the bottom quartile.

- **Customer satisfaction** – improved engagement saw a net promoter score (NPS) score 24 per cent higher than those where engagement had declined. NPS is a key indicator of customer satisfaction, loyalty and positive intent towards a company or brand.

- **Innovation** – 59 per cent of engaged employees say their jobs bring out their most creative ideas vs only 3 per cent of disengaged employees.

- **Absence and well-being** – engaged employees take an average 2.69 sick days per annum vs 6.19 days for the disengaged.

- **Retention** – companies with high levels of engagement show staff turnover rates 40 per cent lower than companies where engagement levels are low. This carries an enormous cost.

- **Health and safety** – organizations with engagement in the bottom quartile average 63 per cent more accidents than those in the top quartile.

When managers begin to reel in these benefits because of higher levels of engagement, the business outcomes flow through in the form of greater customer satisfaction and increased revenues. Because of greater productivity, profitability rises too. Strong teams who foster strong relationships inside and outside the company enable sustainable success.

In country after country, industry after industry, the statistics show the same thing – engagement brings better performance. More and more businesses conduct employee engagement surveys and are attempting to find ways to create conditions where employees do feel more engaged with the company.

So, how engaged are the workforces of the world? According to Gallup, a management consulting company which provides research and consulting to companies around the world, only 15 per cent of the world's employees are truly engaged. Aon Hewitt, another global consulting business, which specializes in employee research, says that engagement levels globally have remained static for years and may even be declining. Their research, among 1,000 organizations around the world employing more than 5 million employees, suggests that only 25 per cent of employees are highly engaged, with 39 per cent moderately engaged.

Admittedly, those two research studies have quite a wide range in their findings, but whatever way you look at it, there are an awful lot of employees out there who are simply not engaged and therefore not performing anywhere near their potential. That suggests companies are spending more time and more money on engagement, but with no improvement in results. So what's the problem?

Everywhere you look, indications are that companies are spending too little time improving the skills of their managers, and focusing on engagement in the wrong ways, so they fail to make any significant difference. Managers account for at least 70 per cent of the variance in employee engagement scores. There is a high correlation between highly engaged employees and highly effective managers. There is also evidence that high standards, results-driven leaders, who at the same time dedicate effort to building engaged and fun-to-work-with teams, are the ones who are most highly rated – by employees.

We spend so much of our lives working – the average person is going to spend between 80,000 and 90,000 hours at work. If most workers of the world are not enjoying their jobs, that's an awful lot of wasted time and minimal effort going into the hugely important task of creating wealth and improving the fortunes of communities all over the world.

We might be forgiven for thinking that this issue of poor engagement is only about employees. Of course, all managers are highly engaged and motivated, are they not? Well, no. In a research project entitled *The State of the American Manager,* Gallup found that across 190 industries, only 35 per cent of managers were actively engaged. Over half did not feel very engaged and 14 per cent were actively poisonous and disengaged.

It goes without saying that this creates a terrible cascade effect – because a manager's engagement or lack of engagement has a direct effect on employees, with dire consequences. Employees supervised by highly engaged managers are 59 per cent more likely to be engaged and high-performing. But two-thirds of managers are not very engaged themselves. On top of that, when managers lack the basic soft skills of leadership as well, it becomes harder and harder to deliver the goals because high levels of disengagement quickly follow.

Which soft skills do employees most want from managers?

It helps to understand which soft skills employees most appreciate in their managers. Are these the same soft skills that do the most to encourage the willingness of employees to go the extra mile? These employees – the ones who are willing to put in additional effort – are the ones who can make or break a company. This is where true competitive edge emerges – in teams where people care more about each other, care more about customers, and care more about outcomes.

Of course, pay matters. So too do working conditions. As does having the right technical skills and tools to do the job. But, in research conducted for me in 2016 by YouGov, the global online research company, the results suggested that the thing that makes the biggest difference to discretionary effort is the soft skills of managers.

In a survey among 4,000 managers and employees, YouGov found that the most important management skills were in the following five areas:

1 the character of the manager;
2 the passion of the manager, and his or her commitment to the cause of the organization;
3 how the manager made employees feel about themselves;
4 the direction given to employees by the manager, with an emphasis on connecting employees to corporate goals and giving regular feedback; and
5 how well and how often a manager communicated with staff.

These closely mirror the five skill sets of charismatic leaders:

1 being able to project an authentic persona, with honesty and integrity;
2 having enough personal power to convince people you are worth following;
3 having the skills to make people feel appreciated and valued;
4 being able to connect people to a compelling purpose; and
5 being a skilled and persuasive communicator.

To help me understand more about which management skills were not only most important to employees, *and* which also had the most impact on employee effort, YouGov looked at 21 behaviours of managers that were observable and measurable, and spoke with 4,000 managers and employees in a wide range of private-sector, public-sector and not-for-profit organizations. In 2019, based on my new understanding of the DNA of charisma, I revisited all of this data and broke it down into the five traits of charismatic leaders. I was able to see how managers rate themselves for charisma. Crucially, I was also able to see how employees rate them.

The most striking point to emerge from the survey was the huge gap between how managers assessed their own skill levels and how employees saw them. Managers routinely overestimated their skills, with the biggest gaps appearing where these skills actually mattered the most (Figure 36.6).

FIGURE 36.6 The charisma gap

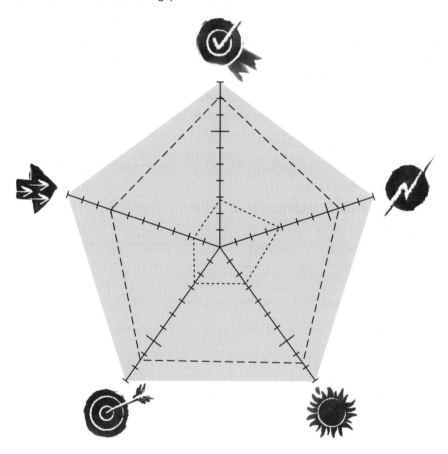

HOW LEADERS ESTIMATED THEMSELVES

HOW EMPLOYEES RATED LEADERS' CHARISMA

Employees simply do not rate their bosses highly for charisma. Where managers and employees come closest is on the trait of personal power. There is most agreement here – that managers do have authority, are passionate and do care about the company's goals. However, managers and employees are furthest apart on the trait of persuasiveness. Here the biggest issue is that managers simply don't show up enough for the critical conversations that drive progress. If you were to do the same charisma test and then ask your employees to rate you, would the same gaps emerge?

How the marking differed between managers and employees

1. Authenticity

Overall, 90 per cent of managers believe they have a strongly authentic persona. They believe absolutely that they have integrity and are sincere. Sadly, only half of employees would agree and nearly a third actively disagree. Among employees who have their doubts about their managers (and there are many) there are likely to be feelings of uncertainty, wariness and even danger. Their managers will appear to them to be unpredictable, hypocritical and insincere. Generally, employees feel their managers have a low level of self-awareness. This is one of the biggest gaps in manager vs employee views in the entire survey! I believe this is mainly because managers will seldom show their vulnerability by talking about their weaknesses, even though research shows that those who do so drive higher levels of loyalty, motivation and effort. When employees feel that their managers are inauthentic, levels of trust will be low, between the manager and his/her team, and between team members. Cooperation and collaboration will suffer, as will innovation.

2. Personal power

Managers rate themselves second lowest overall in the area of personal power, with many displaying a lack of passion for their work, a lack of engagement with their organizational culture and purpose, and a lack of awareness of how their body language affects members of their teams. Inadvertently sending the wrong signals can have devastating effects on team members who draw negative conclusions from those signals. Employees send a sharp warning in this research, with only one in five saying their manager is good at using body language. Ironically, managers overall give themselves almost 7 out of 10 for being personally powerful, and employees give them just under 4 out of 10, which is the smallest gap between manager and employee thinking in this research. Nevertheless, there are still sufficient numbers of employees who question the manager's personal power, to give us pause for thought. For example, a lack of commitment and passion will convey itself to employees and be highly contagious. How can leaders bring out the passion of their team members, if they are unable to show any themselves?

3. Warmth

If an affective presence is about how you make your employees feel, managers are doing a poor job of it, according to the YouGov research. Overall, 9 out of 10 managers think they do enough to make their employees feel valuable and cared for, while as many as 50 per cent of employees feel otherwise. How managers make their team members feel is one of the most important drivers of motivation and effort. Yet this YouGov survey shows this is the area where managers perform the worst, in the eyes of employees. For example, only two out of every five employees say they feel respected at work. Nearly a third say they feel disrespected. There is an enormous cost to these feelings of disrespect, which can spread from employee to employee, and from them to customers. Employees rate this trait of warmth as the single most important in management, and YouGov says it is the biggest contributor to their willingness to put in more discretionary effort.

4. Drive

Goal-setting is rated by employees as the fifth most important behaviour of management, behind attributes such as making them feel important, honesty and sincerity, and consistent principled behaviours. Employees want to have a sense of meaning in their lives and need to know how what they do contributes to the organization's goals. They especially want to know that what the organization does adds value to people's lives and is important work. Constructive feedback is also highly valued, as is having their work recognized and praised. This kind of feedback and praise is best done frequently, but it is one of the areas of management behaviour employees are also critical of. They feel they do not get good enough feedback.

5. *Persuasiveness*

You can see from the charisma gap illustration (Figure 36.6) that employees give their harshest criticism to managers for a lack of effective communication. One in three managers recognize that they are not effective at public speaking, and more than half of employees agree. But employees say that that matters less to them than how often managers turn up to have conversations with them. In the survey, more than half of the employees reported that their manager simply did not communicate with them frequently enough. They wanted managers who could demonstrate that they understand where members of their team were coming from, could talk to them in ways that made sense to them, and could show them that they related to how they are feeling. Sadly, more than 50 per cent of employees said that their manager was bad at connecting with them.

How inspiring are managers?

YouGov also asked managers to rate how inspiring they thought they were. Some 73 per cent thought that they were either extremely or somewhat inspiring. However, when asked to rate how inspiring they thought their managers were, only 41 per cent of employees said their bosses were either extremely or somewhat inspiring. One in three said their bosses were actually demotivating.

The YouGov research demonstrates that when managers are able to drive up the charisma ratings employees give them, it makes a dramatic difference to the willingness of employees to put in extra effort. Charismatic managers can make employees feel more respected by 65 per cent, a major contributor to enhancing their willingness to go that extra mile. If managers can improve their ratings moderately in *all five skill sets,* they can drive up motivation by more than 50 per cent, and increase discretionary effort among employees by 24 per cent, said YouGov.

In spite of the huge difference in opinions between managers and their employees about the effectiveness of their managers, YouGov showed there is a remarkable degree of alignment on what everyone thinks are the most important management behaviours. They are:

1 Making employees feel important and appreciated – 66 per cent of managers and 65 per cent of employees rated this as the most important skill in a manager.

2 Honesty and sincerity – the second most important attribute, with 46 per cent of managers and 52 per cent of employees agreeing.

3 Demonstrating consistent principles – with 41 per cent of managers and 38 per cent of employees agreeing.

4 Listening carefully – 36 per cent of managers and 31 per cent of employees agree.

5 Defining goals – 33 per cent of managers and 29 per cent of employees agree.

6 Commitment to purpose – 32 per cent of managers and 27 per cent of employees.

7 Understanding employees' perspective – 25 per cent of managers and 31 per cent of employees agree.

8 Communicating customer/client expectations – 15 per cent of managers and 12 per cent of employees agree.

Way too often, employees don't get the one thing they want the most – to be recognized for their individual contributions and to be made to feel important and appreciated. Gallup surveys show that employees who receive this recognition on a regular basis, at least once a week, increase their individual productivity, create more loyal and satisfied customers, and are more likely to stay with their organization.

These data-driven insights into the drivers of happier, healthier and more productive teams are key to your effort to improve your charismatic skills. It is clear that you are unlikely to be as good as you think you are. If you are serious about wanting to become a more effective manager, you need to pay a great deal more attention to learning and practising the skills of charisma.

37

How to measure your own charisma and determine your shape

To understand the shape of your charisma and, more importantly, where you most need to improve, you need first to subject yourself to the charisma questionnaire, and then plot your marks onto the charisma measurement tool. Ideally, you should ask colleagues and members of your team to do it as well.

Now, finally, let's make this book all about *you*. Let's look at the shape of your charisma and, more importantly, let's also ask others to assess your skills so that you can understand where you most need to improve. It is highly likely that you're going to assess your skills in each of these key behaviours more generously than members of your team might do.

I have conducted this 'charisma questionnaire' with dozens of leaders and, mostly, their direct reports marked them lower in one or two areas than they did themselves. (It was very seldom that they marked them lower in all five of the traits of charisma.) Occasionally, members of the team marked them higher than they did themselves. Either way, the marks led to some constructive conversations that enabled these leaders to understand more about where they were falling short of expectations, and what specific skills they needed to improve in order to behave in ways that drove up motivation.

To identify the shape of your charisma yourself, you need first to fill out the charisma Self Questionnaire (see Step 1 below). Then ask your team members to do the version of the Employee Questionnaire (see Step 4 below).

Be honest and brutal when you mark yourself, because your employees will, if you ask (and you definitely should!) However, they will most probably only do this if you allow them to fill it in anonymously.

Step 1: Complete the self questionnaire

Turn to Table A.1 in the Appendix, and complete the Self Questionnaire.

Step 2: Plot your charisma shape

When you have completed the questionnaire, plot your marks in red pen on the charisma measurement tool in Figure 37.1, where 0 is at the centre and 10 is at the outer edge.

FIGURE 37.1 The charisma measurement tool

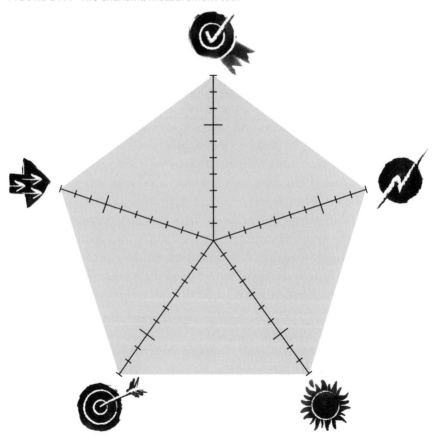

You will now be able to see the shape of your charisma and see where you fall below or above a desirable score of 7 on each axis.

Step 3: Compare your shape with others

Next, compare your mark with those of the 2,000 managers and 2,000 employees YouGov surveyed to see how you would shape up against these ratings (see Figure 37.2). Plot your scores on to this chart, again with a red pen, to see how your shape differs from other managers and from the view of the general population of employees.

Step 4: Plot your employees' marks

Next, ask your employees/colleagues to complete the Employee Questionnaire (Table A.2 in the Appendix). Look at the marks that members of your team have given you, and plot those on both Figures 37.1 and 37.2, this time in blue pen. Try not to be offended if they give you low marks in any area. Their perceptions might be coloured by all sort of factors that have little to do with you. On the other hand, their marks may be an accurate and undiluted view of how they see your behaviours.

Step 5: Understand the gaps

When you have studied the marks and plotted the gaps, talk with members of your team. Show them the aggregated result, not their individual returns, unless they have been happy to give you their feedback and be identified. With their help, try to understand those gaps, and why they have marked you low or high in areas where you rated yourself differently. If need be, drill into each of the five skills in each of the five traits of charisma. Sometimes, gaps can emerge because of differing perceptions about one single poor behaviour. What is it you do or don't do that makes them give you a different mark? (Don't forget to look at where they've marked you higher than you did yourself. Nice! But why? What is it they so value that you must make sure you keep doing?)

FIGURE 37.2 The charisma gap

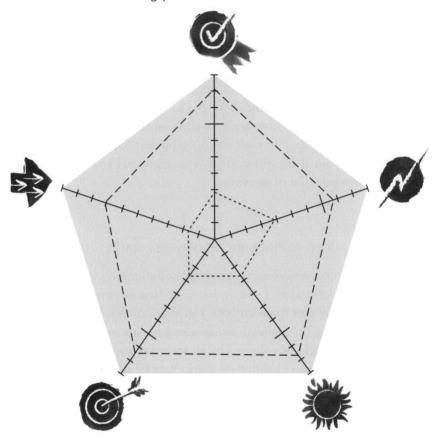

HOW LEADERS ESTIMATED THEMSELVES

HOW EMPLOYEES RATED LEADERS' CHARISMA

Step 6: Get help

Once you have established where the gaps are, get help. Buy other books and read more on each of these skills. Go online and read blogs and advice articles on the subjects where you most want to improve. Do training courses. Get coaching. Whether you pay for your own development or whether you persuade your company to pay, it will be a great investment in your future as a leader.

Your team has more potential than you imagine

The people in your team have far more potential to contribute to your goals than you could ever imagine. As managers, we constantly underestimate what our people are capable of. Employees agree. In fact, as many as two-thirds say that they have more to offer in skills and talent than they are currently being asked to demonstrate at work. Any improvement in engagement levels leads to improvements in performance and then in revenue – often within 12 months.

Your success depends on how engaged every member of your team is. And that depends on how charismatic you are, for charisma builds engagement. If you systematically improve your behaviours by improving your skills for each of the five traits of charisma, you will also improve the engagement, motivation and discretionary effort of every member of your team. With that will come the leap in performance you are seeking, and with that, your future looks bright. Charisma is something you already have – all you have to do is bring it more to the surface, with focus and purpose, and then use it as a positive force for good.

The end.

But, for you, just the beginning...

APPENDIX

The tools

This Appendix contains all the tools you need to drive up your charisma quotient:

- the summaries will remind you of the traits and skills you need to develop;
- the questionnaires can be used to rate yourself or to get your colleagues to rate you on your current leadership charisma;
- the diagrams will give you a visual guide to where you need to improve your skills.

Charisma, summarized

The five traits of charisma

To be more charismatic, leaders need to do five things:

1 They need to let people know who they truly are and win trust. To do this they need the skills that will help them deliver authenticity.

2 They need to command attention and win respect. For this, they need the skills that will help them develop personal power.

3 They need to make people feel good about themselves and that they are an important member of the team. To do this they need to develop the skills that will give them more warmth, and an affective presence.

4 They need to give every member of their team direction and goals. To do this they need to have the skills to articulate a compelling vision and sense of purpose that will arouse the passion to deliver it. They need to have a cause, and the drive to achieve it.

5 They need to be able to connect with employees and enthuse them with the will to succeed. To do this, they need to develop their communication skills and become more persuasive.

In summary, these are the five key traits of charismatic leaders:

1 authenticity;

2 power;

3 warmth;

4 drive;

5 persuasiveness.

The five skills of each charismatic trait

AUTHENTIC

INTEGRITY
VALUES
COMMITMENT
SELF-AWARENESS
HUMILITY

POWERFUL

LEADER MINDSET
POSITIVITY
ENERGY
ASSERTIVENESS
LOOK THE PART

WARM

ENGAGING
GOOD LISTENER
RESPECTFUL
APPRECIATIVE
INCLUSIVE

DRIVEN

COMPELLING CAUSE
CUSTOMER FOCUS
ALIGNS GOALS
EMPOWERING
CONTINUOUS IMPROVER

PERSUASIVE

UNDERSTAND AUDIENCES
GOOD CONVERSATIONALIST
POWERFUL POV
GOOD STORYTELLER
EXCELLENT SPEAKER

To be seen as authentic, leaders must be skilled in the following areas:

1 Delivering honesty and integrity, consistently.

2 Having and living a personal mission and values.

3 Being visibly committed.

4 Being self-aware.

5 Having humility.

To work on your personal power, you need to pay attention to the following behaviours:

1 Displaying a leadership mindset.

2 Being positive and optimistic.

3 Being energetic and passionate.

4 Being assertive.

5 Looking and sounding the part.

To develop warmth and have an affective presence, leaders need to be:

1 More charming and engaging.

2 Better, more attentive and empathetic listeners.

3 More respectful.

4 More appreciative.

5 More inclusive.

To align people to a cause, leaders need to learn how to:

1 Develop and articulate a compelling cause or purpose.

2 Bring customers into every team meeting and decision.

3 Align everyone's goals to a common vision.

4 Deliver autonomy through a freedom framework.

5 Develop a culture of continuous improvement.

To be more persuasive, leaders need to learn how to:

1 Understand their audiences better.

2 Facilitate conversations and encourage debate on difficult issues.

3 Take a stand with a powerful point of view.

4 Tell good stories.

5 Be a good speaker on stage.

The Self Questionnaire

TABLE A.1 Self Questionnaire

The Self Questionnaire
Give yourself a mark out of 10 for each of the statements below, where 0 is terrible, and 10 is excellent.

I am an authentic leader: 🛡️

1	I consistently deliver honesty and integrity.	.../10
2	I have and live a clear personal mission and set of values.	.../10
3	I am visibly committed to our cause, and my team.	.../10
4	I am self-aware.	.../10
5	I am humble.	.../10
	Overall, I have an Authenticity rating of	.../50

Now divide your total mark by 5 and plot on to the chart on the axis for Authenticity.

I have a strong presence and personal power: 💫

1	I take the lead on issues when I need to.	.../10
2	I am consistently positive and optimistic.	.../10
3	I am energetic and passionate.	.../10
4	I am respectfully assertive.	.../10
5	I look and sound like a leader.	.../10
	Overall, I have a Personal Power rating of	.../50

Now divide your total mark by 5 and plot on to the chart on the axis for Personal Power

I have warmth and a positive effect on people: 🌟

1	I am able to engage with people easily.	.../10
2	I am an attentive and empathetic listener.	.../10
3	I am respectful of others.	.../10
4	I am appreciative and praise often.	.../10
5	I am inclusive, in every way.	.../10
	Overall, I have a Warmth rating of	.../50

Now divide your total mark by 5 and plot on to the chart on the axis for Warmth.

I have drive and a cause and can align people to a cause: 🎯

1	I develop and articulate a compelling cause or purpose for my team.	.../10
2	I bring customers into every team meeting and decision.	.../10
3	I align everyone's goals to a common vision.	.../10

(continued)

TABLE A.1 (Continued)

4	I delegate well and allow my employees appropriate autonomy.	.../10
5	I drive for continuous improvement in pursuit of our cause.	.../10
	Overall, I have a Drive rating of	.../50

Now divide your total mark by 5 and plot on to the chart on the axis for Drive.

I am a persuasive leader:

1	I always seek first to understand my audience before communicating.	.../10
2	I facilitate conversations well and encourage debate on difficult issues.	.../10
3	I frequently take a stand with a powerful point of view.	.../10
4	I tell good, purposeful stories.	.../10
5	I am a good speaker on stage.	.../10
	Overall, I have a Persuasiveness rating of	.../50

Now divide your total mark by 5 and plot on to the chart on the axis for Persuasiveness.

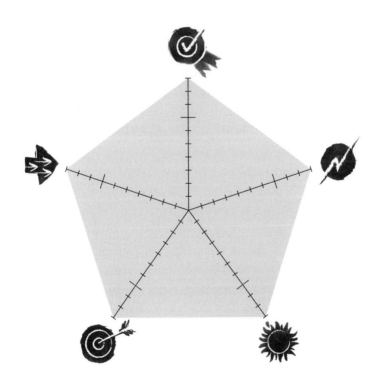

The Employee Questionnaire

TABLE A.2 Employee Questionnaire

The Employee Questionnaire
*Give your manager a mark out of 10 for each of the statements below,
where 0 is terrible and 10 is excellent*

My manager is an authentic leader

1	My manager is honest and has integrity.	.../10
2	He/she lives a clear personal mission and set of values.	.../10
3	My boss is visibly committed to our cause, and our team.	.../10
4	My manager is self-aware.	.../10
5	My manager is humble.	.../10
	Overall, my manager has an Authenticity rating of	.../50

*Now divide your total mark by 5 and plot on to the chart on the
axis for Authenticity.*

My manager has a strong presence and personal power:

1	He/she takes the lead on issues when needed.	.../10
2	My manager is consistently positive and optimistic.	.../10
3	My manager is energetic and passionate.	.../10
4	He/she is respectfully assertive.	.../10
5	He/she looks and sounds like a leader.	.../10
	Overall, my manager has a Personal Power rating of	.../50

*Now divide your total mark by 5 and plot on to the chart on the
axis for Personal Power*

My manager has warmth and a positive effect on people:

1	He/she is able to engage with people easily.	.../10
2	My manager is an attentive and empathetic listener.	.../10
3	My manager is respectful of others.	.../10
4	He/she is appreciative and praises often.	.../10
5	My manager is inclusive, in every way.	.../10
	Overall, my manager has a Warmth rating of	.../50

Now divide your total mark by 5 and plot on to the chart on the axis for Warmth.

My manager is driven and can align people to a cause:

1	My manager has developed and articulated a compelling cause or purpose for my team.	.../10
2	My manager brings customers into every team meeting and decision.	.../10

(continued)

TABLE A.2 (Continued)

3	My manager aligns everyone's goals to a common vision.	.../10
4	He/she delegates well and allows employees appropriate autonomy.	.../10
5	My manager strives for continuous improvement in pursuit of our cause.	.../10
	Overall, my manager has a Drive rating of	.../50

Now divide your total mark by 5 and plot on to the chart on the axis for Drive.

My manager is a persuasive leader: ➥

1	He/she always seeks first to understand me before communicating.	.../10
2	My manager facilitates conversations and encourages debate on difficult issues.	.../10
3	My manager frequently takes a stand with a powerful point of view.	.../10
4	He/she often tells good, purposeful stories that help me understand my job and role.	.../10
5	My manager is a good speaker on stage.	.../10
	Overall, my manager has a Persuasiveness rating of	.../50

Now divide your total mark by 5 and plot on to the chart on the axis for Persuasiveness.

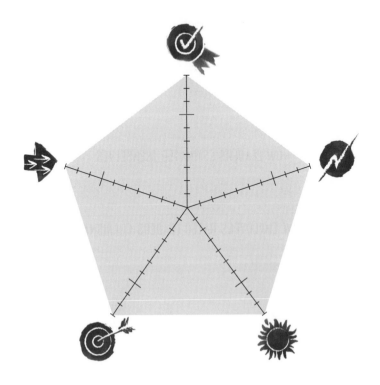

The charisma gap

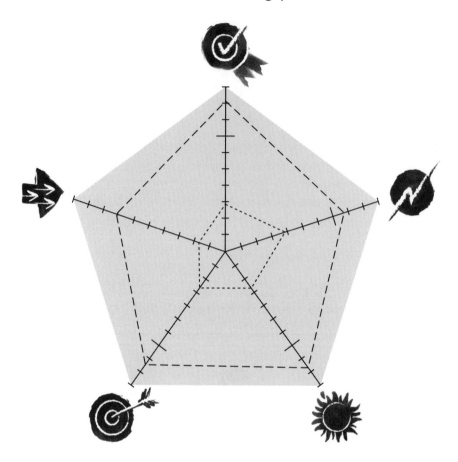

- - - - -

HOW LEADERS ESTIMATED THEMSELVES

- - - - - - - - - -

HOW EMPLOYEES RATED LEADERS' CHARISMA

Balanced charisma

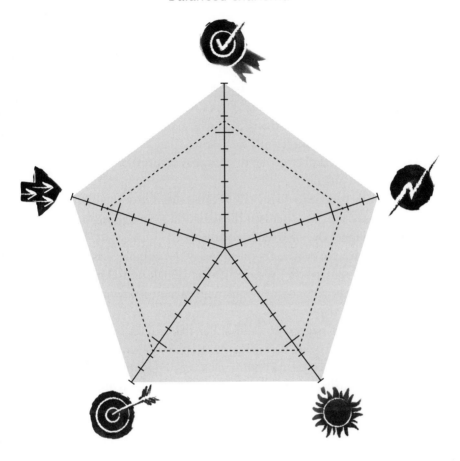

This is the charismatic leader!

ACKNOWLEDGEMENTS

Early in 2018, I was asked to do a webinar for a global financial services company. The organizers told me it was for their senior managers, and that they typically had more than 2,000 who signed up for these leadership webinars – if they were sufficiently interesting. They said that, after advertising a webinar, it normally took up to six weeks before they knew how many managers would attend.

They approached me to do the talk because they knew about my previous books on leadership. We discussed the issues they were facing and decided to call the webinar 'The Charismatic Manager'.

Two days later, the organizers called to say the webinar was already, and amazingly, fully subscribed. Even at my most vainglorious, I would struggle to assert this was because of my popular appeal and renown. It was the title that had attracted them.

To all of those managers, my thanks. You inspired me to write this book, and you gave me the belief that managers all over the world would find the subject of leadership charisma both fascinating and worthwhile.

Writing is a lonely pursuit, once the fun of the research and interviews is over, so special thanks must also go to my band of critics, who dutifully read my early drafts and gave me invaluable advice and encouragement along the way. To Paul Larbey, Lucian Hudson, Andrew Sherville, Ipek Yigit, Vitaly Vasiliev, Jason Murray and Chris Cudmore: I hope you feel I have done your wise words justice.

Thanks to my daughter, Kirstin Kaszubowska, for her inspired idea to develop icons for each of the traits of charisma, and for her early sketches. These were brilliantly brought to life by Matthew Gould, an illustrator it has been my pleasure to work with in the past.

Thank you also to the dozens of leaders who tested the test for me, and willingly subjected themselves to the views of their direct reports, and the testing conversations that followed. Again, your feedback was unbelievably helpful.

Finally, thanks again to the team at Kogan Page, for all your work to get this book on to the shelves. It is our fourth book together, testimony to a long and successful partnership.

PS: This is my fifth book. My wife, Liz, now knows only too well that moment when I go into what she politely calls 'book writing mode'. What she means is that I become selfishly and myopically focused on what I am doing, and she has to pick up the considerable slack that follows. Thank you, my love. I know I couldn't have achieved anything in my life, if not for you.

ABOUT THE AUTHOR

Kevin Murray specializes in helping leaders to be more effective and inspiring.

He has been advising leadership teams for three decades, and has worked across a wide variety of sectors, helping those leaders to deal with significant change programmes and other business challenges including, sometimes, managing crises.

He has also provided personal coaching for many of those leaders and worked with them to create greater strategic alignment among their top managers, and more engaged staff.

He is author of the best-selling books *The Language of Leaders*, *Communicate to Inspire*, and *People with Purpose*, all of which were published by Kogan Page and are now on sale in many languages around the world.

Kevin has interviewed more than 120 CEOs for his research and has commissioned several groundbreaking studies to understand what most inspires employees. As a result of his books and research, Kevin now gives talks and workshops on leadership around the world.

He was himself a successful businessman, having – for 20 years – led the companies in the public relations division of Chime Communications, a global communications group. He has 46 years of experience in communications and business, first as a journalist, then in corporate communications, and finally in consultancy. He was Director of Communications for British Airways, and before that Director of Corporate Affairs for the United Kingdom Atomic Energy Authority (AEA).

He started his career in 1973 as a crime reporter on *The Star* newspaper in South Africa, and has also written a chart-topping crime novel, *Blood of The Rose*.

For more information, visit www.leadershipcommunication.co.uk.

INDEX